The Heath with the Birches

A History of Birkenhead

by

Agnes L. McCulloch

*To Dorothy,
with best wishes,
Agnes*

To my Parents
Margaret and John L. McCulloch

CONTENTS

		Page
Chapter 1	The Priory	1
Chapter 2	The Years Between	9
Chapter 3	A Town is Born	15
Chapter 4	New Ventures	28
Chapter 5	Financial Recovery and Progress	43
Chapter 6	The 20th Century	61
Chapter 7	Personalities	78
Chapter 8	Facts and Figures	87
Bibliography		92

First published 1991 by Countyvise Limited, 1 & 3 Grove Road, Rock Ferry, Birkenhead, Wirral, Merseyside L42 3XS.

Copyright © Agnes L. McCulloch, 1991.

Photoset and printed by Birkenhead Press Limited, 1 & 3 Grove Road, Rock Ferry, Birkenhead, Wirral, Merseyside L42 3XS.

ISBN 0 907768 46 6

All rights reserved. No part of this publication may be reproduced, stored in a retrieval system, or transmitted, in any form, or by any means, electronic, chemical, mechanical, photocopying, recording or otherwise, without the prior permission of the publisher.

1

The Priory

1066 is probably the most readily remembered date in English history. On the 14th October of that year, William of Normandy defeated King Harold at the battle of Hastings, and the course of English history was changed.

William proceeded to London and after the surrender of the city he was duly crowned King of England and is still remembered as William the Conqueror. It must not be assumed that the English people welcomed William and his Norman followers. Led by many of the Saxon nobles there was fierce resistance to him in many parts of the country which William quelled, often with great cruelty, and so his followers progressed in all directions throughout the realm subduing opposition and confiscating the lands and possessions of the Saxons. William personally led many of these battles and after he had successfully subdued York, advanced on Chester.

Chester in the 11th Century was of primary importance, both commercially and strategically. It was the most important port in the north west and the gateway to Wales. The river Dee was wide and navigable and centuries earlier the Romans had recognised its significance by establishing a settlement there. Chester surrendered without resistance and following his usual custom, William built a strong fortress there, repaired the existing walls and created one of his followers, Walter de Gherbaud, Earl of Chester. Leaving Walter to maintain law and order he returned to Winchester having subdued the entire country from north to south.

Walter de Gherbaud, weary of fighting, soon returned home and William made his nephew Hugh, known as the Wolf or Hugh Lupus, the new Earl of Chester. Hugh Lupus had distinguished himself in battle and was a young man of great promise and obvious potential. The blade of his sword, now in the British Museum, is four feet long and the weapon is so heavy that it requires both hands of a very strong man to wield it. His uncle, as a further mark of his favour, made Chester a county Palatine thus making him a feudal lord with supreme judicial authority.

Hugh Lupus lived in almost regal splendour. He was immensely powerful and although Chester was remote from William's court he did not lack the luxuries of life. Into the port came spices and other luxuries from the East, wine from France and Spain, cloth from Flanders, linen from Germany, yarn from Ireland, iron from Furness and herrings from Ireland and Scotland. The river Dee also provided a plentiful supply of fish and there was no shortage of corn or meat. Nevertheless, his appointment was no sinecure. The English were unfriendly and the marauding Welsh caused further problems.

Previous to the coming of the Normans, the English and Welsh had fought each other, but a common cause will often unite former enemies and so the Welsh, guerilla fighters of the 11th Century, united with the English against the conquerors and to assist him to combat this local warfare the Earl created seven Norman Barons. Each was given generous grants of land and took his title from his chief place of residence and together with other Barons and several ecclesiastics formed a local parliament for the county of Chester. One of these Barons was Hamon de Massie, Baron Dunham. He held his barony by military service being bound to attend the King with his military forces in defence of the city and county of Chester.

It is interesting to note that the Normans considered the building of churches and endowment of religious houses estimable virtues and after the battle of Hastings the Conqueror established an abbey at Battle, the actual site of the conflict, and he let it be widely known among his followers that he wished them to follow his example and establish religious houses on the lands so generously given to them, but it was Hamon de Massie, the third Baron Dunham, who in 1150 decided to establish a religious house in Wirral. He chose for its site a wooded headland on the River Mersey. The headland was formed by Tranmere Pool to the south and Wallasey Pool to the north and because it was well covered with birch trees was known as Birchen Head or the headland with the birches. Many historians think this was the origin of the name Birkenhead, although some consider the name derives from the head of the Birket river. We cannot be certain, but it is possible that the name comes from the two words birch and heafod. Heafod is an old Norse word meaning head or headland and the two combined give birch-heafod or the headland with the birches.

In 1115 the Baron Halton had founded a priory for the Augustinian Order at Runcorn from which the monks moved to a new site at Norton in 1134. The Birkenhead priory was founded in 1150 and was followed by another religious house established in 1178 by John 6th Baron Halton at Stanlow. The Stanlow site was not well chosen and, because it was subject to severe flooding, the community of Cistercian monks moved from there to Whalley in Lancashire in 1294. So in barely more than sixty years, three monastic houses were

The Priory ruins with Saint Mary's tower in the background.

established on the Cheshire side of the Mersey. This religious zeal was probably inspired by the new mood of piety which was prominent in Europe at that time and which was expressed in tangible form by the Crusades or holy wars.

The Birkenhead priory was a small religious house. It provided for sixteen Benedictine monks, and since it was independent, had the priviledge of electing its own prior. It was also richly endowed by Hamon de Massie with lands at Bidston, Backford, Moreton, Tranmere, Claughton, Over Bebington and Saughall Massie, plus fishing rights half way across the Mersey. A further concession gave the right to hold a court of the Manor of Claughton.

The total population of Wirral, at that time, was small and was mostly concentrated along the coast where the chief occupation was fishing. There were a few farms, but the land was well wooded and in the early 12th Century became a Royal Hunting Forest. The Wirral Horn dates from this period and was the badge of office given by Randal de Meschines, Earl of Chester, to Alan Sylvestre when he appointed him Chief Forrester or Bailiff of the Forest of Wirral. Sylvestre was also given the manors of Puddington and Storeton and chose to live at Storeton Hall. The Horn passed through the female

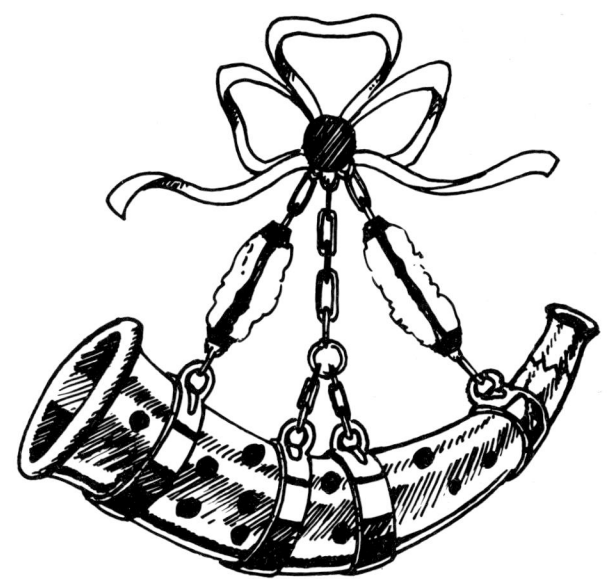

line to the Bamvilles and the Stanleys and is now in the possession of the Earl of Cromer. It is described as being slightly curved and tipped with brass at the small end. It is nearly seventeen inches long, yellowish brown in colour and spotted in shades of blue and black.

The monks and their helpers were probably the only occupants of the headland and apart from their religious duties they had three main occupations. They farmed their land, ferried passengers to Liverpool and cared for travellers unable to cross the Mersey through adverse weather conditions. Their nearest farm was the Grange at Claughton and to reach it they followed a lane which led from the Priory past Tranmere Pool and then along the bank of a small river known, in the 19th century, as the Rubicon, although the origin of the name is obscure. The river flowed through a pleasantly wooded valley between Tranmere Hill and the high ground connecting Storeton and Oxton and with this pleasant valley on their left, their way led along what is now Grange Road, Grange Road West and Grange Mount, to the farm which was situated about Alfred Road. The lane they followed was also used by travellers using the ferry and it branched to the left at what is now Charing Cross, crossing the river to join Whetstone Lane on the opposite bank. This seemingly roundabout route was necessary for travellers to and from Chester because the Tranmere Pool extended inland as far as the present Central Station, where at high tide it became a wide expanse of water. The river Rubicon also proved an obstacle since it widened before flowing into Tranmere Pool. Therefore travellers were obliged to skirt the Pool by using Tranmere Hill, or as we know it Holt Hill, to enable them to reach the Old Chester Road on the far side.

In 1207 King John, needing a safe anchorage for his ships in his warfare against the Welsh and Irish, chose Liverpool for this purpose and declared it a Royal Borough. He granted the Burgesses a weekly market, an annual fair and the right to ferry passengers to Birkenhead. It is possible that he also envisaged the building of the castle, but it was not until 1235 that Liverpool Castle, a stone structure, was completed.

The markets and fairs proved a great attraction to the people in Cheshire. There was also the movement of troops and the monks at the Priory therefore found the number of passengers using the ferry was greatly increased. The ferry boats must have been very cumbersome craft. They were rowing boats with sails and their safe passage was influenced by tide, wind and current. Ferry tolls from Birkenhead were:- foot passengers one half penny or one farthing on market days. A man with a pack one penny and a man with an unladen horse also one penny, but a man with a laden horse was two

The Chapter House Birkenhead Priory. (Courtesy Williamson Art Gallery). The chapel has been in use from c.1150 to the present day.

pence. A quarter of grain cost one penny. Examples of goods carried include:- bacon pigs, sheep and sheepskins, rabbit, fox and squirrel skins, worsted yarn, fish, salmon, honey, wine, sea coals, iron, horse shoes, onions, millstones, brushwood and tin. These goods give a revealing insight into the occupations of the local rural community. The ferry tolls listed were not paid without criticism and the Prior was accused of excessive charges. In 1354 he was summoned before the Earl of Chester's court to answer the accusations made against him, but he successfully defended himself and the case was dismissed.

In 1275 Edward I stayed at the Priory and two years later in 1277, while preparing a campaign against the Welsh, he returned and this second visit lasted for five days. It was a very notable occasion during which he received a group of important persons from Scotland. He was accompanied by members of his court, servants, horsemen and wagons and they probably came across Tranmere Hill from Chester.

By 1318 the monks had problems, their accommodation for travellers was inadequate and so they petitioned the King for permission to build a guest house and to charge for food and lodging. Their request was approved and they were granted a Royal Charter. In 1330 they again petitioned the King and were granted another Royal Charter giving them sole rights to ferry passengers to Liverpool. The granting of this second charter is commemorated by a tapestry in the Williamson Art Gallery.

In 1362 the disafforestation of Wirral took place and this meant that farms could be extended and therefore more produce and passengers crossed the Mersey to the Saturday markets in Liverpool. The monks also took their produce to Liverpool and established a granary there in Water Street in which to store their surplus grain between market days.

For almost another two hundred years the monks continued their busy but peaceful way of life and the population of Birkenhead remained so small it could hardly be described as a hamlet. Then in 1536 came the dissolution of the monasteries.

Henry VIII had financial difficulties. Throughout his reign he wasted vast sums of money on continuous wars. He also wasted his income on building unnecessary palaces. At the time of his death he owned forty houses in different parts of the country and the drain on his resources was enormous. So it was not surprising that he viewed the yearly income of the Church with envy. The churches and religious houses had been richly endowed centuries earlier and the total revenues they received from their lands greatly exceeded the

King's income from the Crown lands. Therefore, after he had severed links with Rome and declared himself Head of the Church in England, he was ready to lay claim to all Church property and began a systematic takeover of religious houses beginning with the smaller ones. Thus in 1536 began the act of plunder known as the dissolution of the monasteries and the Priory in Birkenhead was one of the first to be dissolved. The monks were dispossessed. The Prior was given a pension of twelve pounds a year, but the fate of the other monks is uncertain since accounts differ from a gift of forty shillings and a new gown to an annual pension of five or six pounds a year. Certainly their ordered way of life was over and they were left to fend for themselves.

The King's agents stripped the monastic houses of all valuables, even the lead from the rooftops was removed and sold. The plate was eventually melted down and made into coins and the profits from these spoils gave an instant supply of money, but it was the acquisition of the yearly revenues which had primarily prompted the King's action since even the confiscation of the lesser monasteries produced a new income for the Crown of some £32,000 per year.

Henry did not enjoy this new regular income for very long. To satisfy his constant need for money the sale of land began almost at once, reaching a peak between 1544-45, to provide for the wars with France and Scotland. The landed gentry benefited most from this transfer of land. Existing estates were extended and younger sons had the opportunity to become landowners by acquiring their own estates. In this category Ralph Worsley was a typical example. He was the third son of William Worsley of Worsley in Lancashire and had been a page at the court of Henry VIII. In 1544 he bought the Priory and all lands pertaining to it in the county of Cheshire and thus became Lord of the Manor of Claughton and owner of the headland, together with the ferry boat, the boat house and the ferry rights. The Priory had been partially destroyed at the time of the dissolution, but the chapter house remained intact and was used as a private chapel. More than four centuries later it is still used for weekly services. Records show that Ralph Worsley paid five hundred and sixty eight pounds, eleven shillings and six pence for his new domain and so nearly four hundred years after its foundation the Priory passed into secular hands.

2

The Years Between

After the Priory passed into the possession of Ralph Worsley, little is recorded about the headland and its new occupants. As well as making use of the Chapter House apparently some of the Priory buildings were adapted for domestic use. Judging by the number of Royal appointments held by Ralph Worsley he obviously enjoyed the King's favour and is also reputed to have been interested in the administration of his lands and his rights as Lord of the Manor. In 1550 he fought a successful legal battle with the Lord of Tranmere who had inaugurated a rival ferry at Seacombe. Worsley claimed the loss of valuable revenue and the rights of ferriage by Royal Charter. The Seacombe ferry was therefore discontinued. He died in 1573 aged 80 years leaving three daughters. Alice the eldest inherited her father's property in Cheshire after the deaths of her two sisters. She married Thomas Powell of Horsley in Denbighshire and Thomas Powell is remembered because he began to ferry passengers from Liverpool thus infringing the Liverpool Charter of ferriage. This charter was upheld by law and his attempt to extend his activities on the river ended. He died in 1628 and it was his grandson, Sir Thomas Powell, who built a new house on the site of the old guest house. It appears to have been known as Birket Hall or sometimes the Priory.

The effects of the Civil War reached Birkenhead when, in 1643, Royalist troops occupied Birket Hall and the woods surrounding it. The ferry was an important link across the river to Liverpool and the castle had passed from Royalist to Parliamentary hands a number of times when, in 1644, Cromwell's troops were the victors and in the same year the Royalists in Birkenhead were defeated. It is a long held belief that Cromwell's troops halted on Tranmere Hill whence they opened fire on the headland. The hall was partially destroyed and Tranmere Hill became known as Holt Hill, derived apparently from Halt Hill. Subsequently the hall was rebuilt.

The properties thus restored remained in the Powell family until the end of the century when the second baronet died without a male heir and, in 1713, the estates were sold to John Cleveland of Liverpool. He showed his interest in the ferry by building a new quay on the site later occupied by the lairages, and a boathouse. The boathouse stood behind the quay in a cluster of trees and he refused to allow the Liverpool ferry boats to land there, so the rivalry between the ferries obviously still existed. At that time, there were three ferry boats with four ferry men, six on Saturdays, each earning five shillings per week. There was also a Ferry Master. John Cleveland died in 1716 and in 1724 his estates passed to his daughter Alice who had married Francis Price. The ferry rights thus passed into the Price family who leased them to tenants for the next 120 years. During this period the site of John Cleveland's ferry became known as Woodside.

Over the centuries, Liverpool's fortunes had ebbed and flowed, but from the middle of the 17th Century its importance as a port increased. Tobacco and cotton became major imports and in 1709 work began on the first dock. It was known as the Old Dock and was completed in 1715. Also about that time, Queen Anne granted a charter for a weekly market and fortnightly cattle market on Wednesdays. The cattle market had more than local importance. In the first decade of this century drovers were still bringing their cattle from as far afield as Scotland to the Liverpool markets.

It is not surprising, therefore, that John Cleveland, who was a Member of Parliament for Liverpool, saw the possibilities for the future improved facilities at the ferry to cope with a greater number of passengers. His foresight was justified because in 1737 Liverpool's second dock, the Salthouse, was built and the town across the Mersey began to emerge as a major port. Ferry traffic increased and by 1762 a six-horse coach ran from Woodside to Chester, via Parkgate, three times a week. Its route lay along Grange Road, Whetstone Lane, Church Road, calling at the Black Horse Inn, and Dacre Hill where it joined the Old Chester Road. In 1773 the passing of the Turnpike Act encouraged road construction and repair and in 1786 the Old Chester Road was made into a Turnpike Road and the old rough roadway became a main highway. Four years later, an embankment was built across Tranmere Pool joining the Old Chester Road to Birkenhead. This eliminated the journey across Tranmere Hill and when the route thus became shorter and more comfortable, the number of passengers increased and coaches began to run regularly along the improved roads to a waiting boat at Woodside Ferry where the boathouse had become an inn and coaching station. Originally the coaches did not travel along Chester Street. In her memoirs Harriet Salt describing Birkenhead in the 1820's tells us, "The old turnpike road from Woodside to Chester ran close to the river, through what afterwards became the garden of Mersey Cottage (her home), past the gates of Ivy Rock and along Abbey Street, past the Old Barn and round by Tranmere Pool."

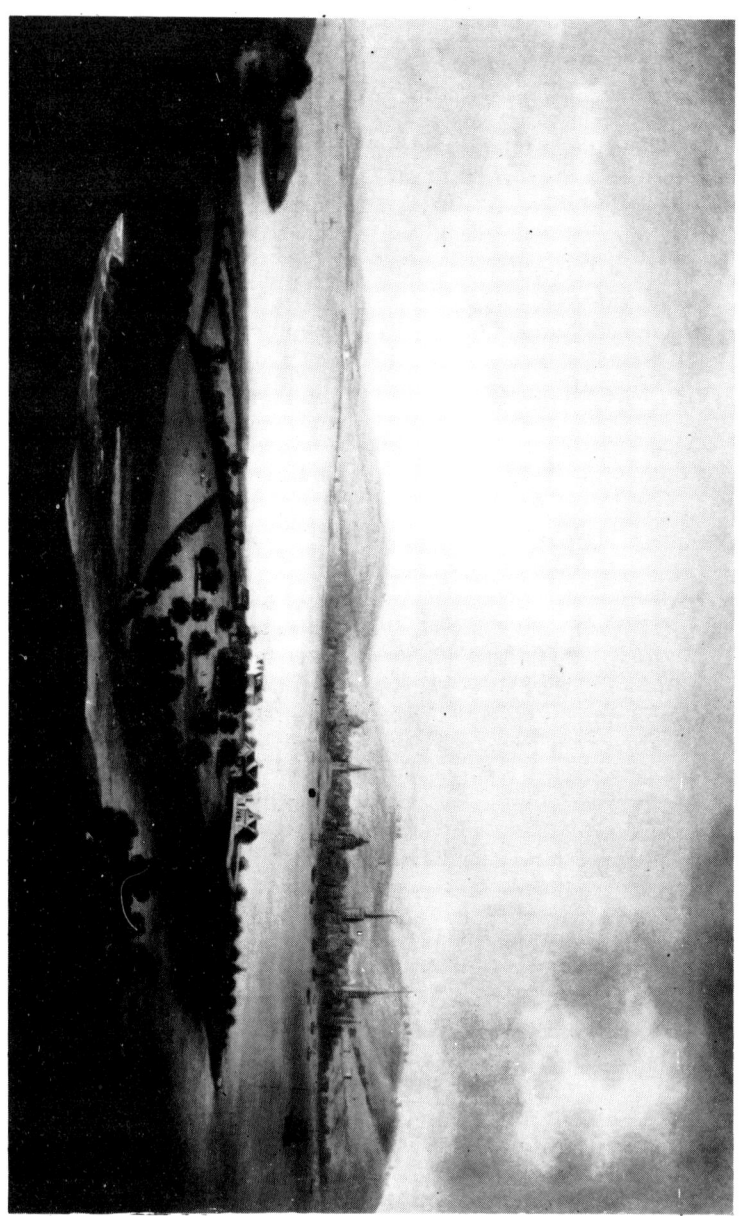

The Headland from Tranmere Hill 1/67 – Charles Eyes. (Courtesy Williamson Art Gallery). Tranmere Pool is shown in the foreground with Wallasey Pool to the north. 18th century Liverpool is depicted across the river.

Liverpool was expanding rapidly, the ferries were busy but the population on the headland remained small.

People passed through Birkenhead but did not stay and, as the 18th Century drew to a close, it was still a small hamlet with just over 100 people who did not enjoy the basic amenities of a village. There was an inn, but no church, street or shop. The chapter house was used as a place of worship on Sundays, but was served from Bidston and later Wallasey. Yet outside influences were at work which, in forty years time, would result in a population of more than 8,000 people.

Fortunately, contemporary descriptions, drawings and paintings make it possible to form a mental picture of the headland and its surroundings before its rural character was completely changed.

The Price family lived in the Hall beside the Priory which was surrounded by gardens where lawns and spinneys stretched down to the rocks on the river front. The red sandstone of the headland contrasting with a beach of golden sand where seaweed covered the rocks and periwinkles and other marine life lived in the pools. Adjoining the Hall was the Birket Hall Farm which stood among trees and had many outbuildings notably the old barn which was blown down in the great gale of 1839. Bridge End Farm was the only other farm on the headland. It was situated near Wallasey Pool, about the present Rendel Street entrance to the tunnel and near it were a number of workmen's cottages and a forge, with cottages for the boatmen on the river front near the ferry. Altogether there were sixteen houses in an area of some 543 acres and since the Hall, the two farms and the Boathouse Inn accounted for four, there were no more than a dozen other dwellings. The land was poor and not suitable for agricultural purposes yet, visually, the prospect must have been pleasing since it comprised woodland, scrubland, open fields and in the area now the park, marshland. The river and the two inlets gave a background of water on three sides and to the south and west the low lying fields gave way to higher ground. To the south Tranmere Hill, crowned by its distinctive mill, rose steeply from Tranmere Pool and through the pleasantly wooded valley between Tranmere Hill and Oxton Hill the river Rubicon wound its way into the pool.

Being in an elevated position in Claughton the Grange Farm, formerly the monk's farm, would have been visible from the headland and further to the west the position of Claughton Farm would have been identified by the forest of Scots Pine trees, hence Forest Road, adjacent to it. Between the two farms two brooks rising in the high ground of Oxton joined, about the present Devonshire Road, and formed a stream which flowed down, in the vicinity of the present Palm Grove, into the marshy land now the Park. To the north west was the village of Claughton and Sharp's House Farm, which stood on the site now occupied by Park High School, and on the lower slopes of Bidston Hill stood Toad Hole Farm, situated about the middle of what is now Bidston Avenue. The ridge of high ground, the Oxton Ridge, would have been a continuous background of woods and heathland with the mill and lighthouse on Bidston outstanding landmarks. Two other small rivers no doubt added interest to the view. The Gill Brook rose about Toad Hole Farm and flowed through a pretty, wooded dale across the middle of the present Laird Street into Wallasey Pool, and from the marsh land by the present Park Entrance the Bridge End Brook wound its way along what is now Conway Street and curved between the present Camden and Adelphi Streets to flow into Wallasey Pool by Bridge End Farm.

The area now the Park sustained brushwood and plants peculiar to marshy districts and was the home of wild duck, but wildlife was plentiful and varied in Wirral including foxes, hares, rabbits, and badgers with otters in the Fender and Birket rivers. Red squirrels lived in the woods and roach, tench and eels were plentiful in the rivers and ponds, while pheasants were found in Prenton and on Tranmere Hill.

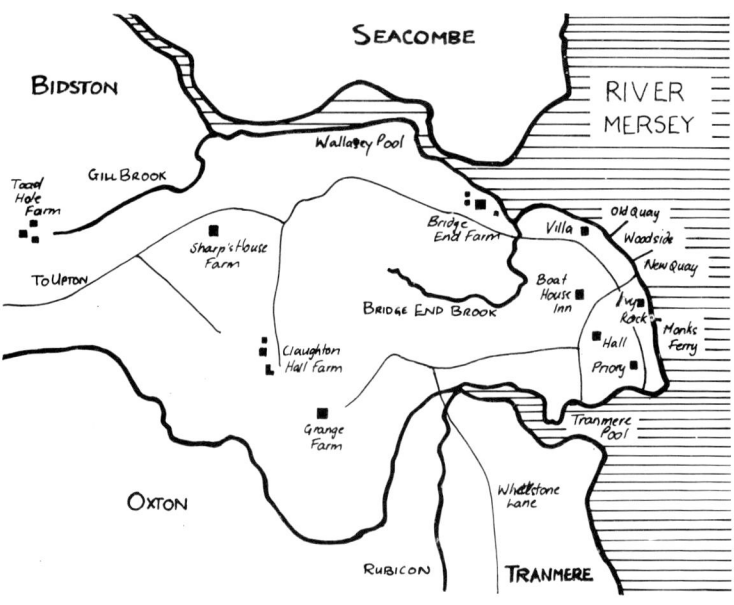

13

It is not surprising, therefore, that the merchants of Liverpool looked across the Mersey to Wirral and seeing the rural charms of Birkenhead considered it would be an attractive alternative to the busy streets and docksides where they lived and worked, but the river and its uncertain and uncomfortable crossing deterred any would-be commuters.

3

A Town Is Born

The census returns for 1801 show that 110 people lived in Birkenhead. There were seventeen families in the sixteen houses. In contrast, Tranmere had a population of 353, Claughton 67, Oxton 137 and Bidston 199. By the next census in 1811 there were only 105 people in eighteen families, listed as 52 males and 53 females. Four were engaged in trade, seven in agriculture and seven more were either fishermen or boatmen. The uneventful way of life which had prevailed for centuries seemed set to continue.

Liverpool in contrast had continued to develop during the latter half of the 18th century and was rapidly becoming a port of primary importance. With the gradual silting up of the River Dee Chester's prominence as a port had declined until by 1810 the Irish packet boat from Parkgate had to be discontinued because of the receding tides, but in Liverpool construction work on the docks had continued from 1761 and this led to such increased activity that for the greater safety of shipping, four lighthouses were erected, two at Mockbeggar and two at Hoylake and in 1771 the Dock Committee began building the Bidston lighthouse which some time later became an important signalling station for ships approaching the Mersey. The Industrial Revolution was also gathering momentum and the development of canals added to Liverpool's trade and prosperity. In 1767 the Bridgewater Canal joined Manchester to Liverpool and in 1771 the Grand Trunk Canal joined Staffordshire to the Mersey.

The Lancashire cotton industry was expanding rapidly. In 1764 James Hargreaves had invented the spinning jenny and later inventions further improved methods in spinning and weaving. Machines were originally worked by water power, but in the 1780s James Watt's steam engine completely changed the industry which moved from water to coal. Large factories were built and the raw cotton was imported through Liverpool mainly from the West Indies, Brazil and India, but the available supply did not meet the demands of the manufacturers.

The type of cotton grown in the Southern States of America was not suitable for export since it was difficult to separate the seeds from the fibres until, in 1793, Eli Whitney invented a cotton gin which cleaned the raw cotton quickly and efficiently and from then onwards cotton was grown in the Southern States in large quantities and its import through the port of Liverpool caused a dramatic increase in the Lancashire cotton industry. The owners of the cotton plantations became prosperous, but the shortage of local labour was acute and so began the infamous slave trade which provided cheap labour for the cotton fields and Liverpool increased its prosperity by capturing a major part of this trade.

Very few slaves came to Liverpool since a three way system was employed. Lancashire cotton and Midland industrial products were exported from Liverpool to Africa where they supplied a ready market. There they were exchanged for slaves who were taken to the West Indies and America and exchanged for sugar and tobacco which was then brought to Liverpool.

Thus the Liverpool merchants prospered and the port continued to grow in importance. Many of the merchants lived over their business premises, since because of the river frontage, the rapidly growing town could only expand inland and this meant a considerable distance lay between the new residential areas on the outskirts of the town and the commercial centre. Then in 1815 a small paddle boat, the Elizabeth, steamed up the Mersey to the bathing resort of Runcorn. She was the first steamship ever to sail on the Mersey and the idea of steam ferry boats was born. For the affluent merchants crossing the river to live in Birkenhead was no longer a pleasant but impractical idea. Within a very few years it was to become a reality.

In 1810 one new resident, possibly taking advantage of the improved roads, had arrived on the headland. Doctor Rowland came from Chester and having bought a cottage and land he built himself a large house on the river bank, near Monks Ferry, calling it Ivy Rock. He had the distinction of being the first newcomer to own land and a substantial property on the headland since Ralph Worsley acquired the Priory in 1544 for himself and his descendants, for by 1818, apart from the cottages and farms there were still only four notable houses in Birkenhead, the Priory or Birket Hall, the house Sir Richard Puleston, a member of the Price family, lived in, Ivy Rock and the old Boathouse Inn.

In 1817, two years after the Elizabeth made her historic passage up the Mersey, the first steam ferry, the Etna, sailed on Whit Monday from the Queens Dock in Liverpool to the Tranmere jetty and the journey took 15 minutes. Coaches were already running daily from the jetty to Chester and Wales and so the journey from Liverpool, via Tranmere, to Chester and beyond grew in popularity and the number of passengers using Woodside declined.

Until 1819 the only landing place at Woodside was the old quay built by John Cleveland about 1714, which was described as being built of boulders and planks. At low tide the sailors often had to take off their shoes and stockings and help passengers to land by carrying them on their backs to the slipway, but in 1819 Francis Price built a bigger, more substantial pier suitable for the new ferry boats and in 1821 Joseph Harrison, a Forwarding Agent in Liverpool, became Birkenhead's first commuter. He purchased land from Francis Price on the river front, later Church Street, and built a house for his family called Mersey Cottage. Evidently in 1821 the steam ferry service from Woodside had not commenced because his daughter relates how he crossed to Liverpool daily at 7 am in the open sailing boat with the guard from the Royal Mail coach. He must have enjoyed living in Birkenhead because he was willing to accept the disadvantages of a crossing which was often very rough and unpleasant. His daughter, Harriet Salt, also relates with wry humour that her father expected the whole family to join him for breakfast every morning and this very early rising caused domestic problems and was certainly not popular in Mersey Cottage.

The new steam ferry service opened up the prospects for urban development and between 1817 and 1818 a firm of developers, Messrs. Hetherington and Grindrod, obviously realising the future possibilities, purchased from Francis Price a considerable amount of land along the river front and around the Priory. The Price family no longer occupied the Hall which was rented to tenants. Mortimer tells us. "In their agreement with Mr. Price it was stipulated that certain streets should be cut through the fields and a new church built by that gentleman; they on the other hand engaging to form another landing place and to construct an hotel on that part of the property now occupied by the Birkenhead Hotel and ferry". These were located at the bottom of Mersey Street. The Birkenhead Hotel was designed to cater for the needs of the more affluent type of residents the new developers hoped to attract. It had a pleasant rural setting on the river front with extensive grounds laid out as ornamental gardens, tea gardens, arbours and a bowling green with a belt of old oak trees providing an outstanding feature. Inside it was well appointed and visitors could enjoy hot, cold and shower baths. Private sitting rooms were available and a billiard room. As a further advantage the stage coach Hirondelle started from the Hotel and conveyed its patrons to Shrewsbury, Newton, Parkgate and Chester. It was later well patronised by Liverpool and Chester county people and became a centre for the local hunting fraternity with a reputation for excellent club dinners. Francis Price built the new church, Saint Mary's, beside the Priory ruins in a setting of open fields. It had an elegant tower and

The old Town Hall, Hamilton Street, c.1833 – W. G. Herdman.
(Courtesy Williamson Art Gallery).

spire with a peal of six bells which could be heard across the whole township. The foundation stone was laid in 1819 and it was opened in 1822. The Reverend Edward Newton continued to serve Birkenhead although he resided and did duty at Wallasey. He had provided Sunday services in the Priory chapel for nearly forty years and it is recorded that he often had to walk from Wallasey and sometimes even wade through Wallasey Pool, where he probably used the stepping stones. He was a devoted man who conducted three services each Sunday; Birkenhead in the morning, Bidston in the afternoon and Wallasey in the evening. His duties were made easier when the Reverend Andrew Knox joined him in 1828 as curate, succeeding him, after his death six years later, as vicar.

Meanwhile, further buildings were being erected and by 1823 when Francis Price's agent, William Lawton, made his survey and map it showed 61 houses and other dwellings while the value of the township was assessed at £3101.

By 1824 people began to occupy the pleasant villas at the water's edge. These early houses were built with the distinctive creamy white stone from the Storeton quarry and there was no shortage of red sandstone for further development since there were no less than five quarries between Storeton and Flaybrick. The other three being at Prenton, Oxton and Tranmere.

In 1824 William Laird came from Liverpool and purchased land from Francis Price at Wallasey Pool which included part of the Bridge End Farm. There he established the boiler and iron shipbuilding yard which was to become the town's main industry and lived conveniently near the yard in a house, with a pleasant garden, in Cathcart Street. The farm continued to provide produce for the local residents for many years until industry finally claimed the land. Nearby stood a pretty villa surrounded by a large garden in which lived a family called Russell. This house later became the Dock Hotel.

Building continued and the population increased rapidly so that in 1828 an article in the Liverpool Mercury stated:- "Woodside: This pleasant village is rapidly rising into eminence and may, at no very distant period, become of considerable importance, if not as a watering place, at least as a favourite sojourn of the merchants of Liverpool".

The semi-rural life obviously appealed to the new residents. The emerging town looked across open country towards the surrounding villages and since there were no buildings to interrupt the view the flags from the signalling station on Bidston Hill were easily identified from the river front. Henry Kelsall Aspinall was born in Birkenhead in 1824 and in his reminiscences published in 1903 he gives a vivid picture of the early town and its later development. His father was John Aspinall, a ship owner, who moved from Liverpool to Birkenhead for the fox-hunting and he tells us. "This was the immediate cause of my father's removing to the Cheshire side of the Mersey. He was one of the first gentlemen resident in Birkenhead." Their house stood near Saint Mary's and a large green field with tall trees lay between it and the river bank. Nearby were the stocks. Twice in the season the Hooton foxhounds met in this field and the huntsmen breakfasted with John Aspinall.

William Laird's shipyard prospered and in 1828 he received his first order for an iron ship. It was a lighter of sixty tons for the Irish lakes named the Wye, but he was also interested in urban development and for this purpose had purchased a considerable amount of land in the centre of the town. In 1826 he entrusted his plans to develop this area to Gillespie Graham who based his designs on the style of architecture popular in his native Edinburgh and it is to him we owe Hamilton Square which is one of the finest of its type in the country. He also planned the grid system of wide straight streets which have always been an outstanding feature of the town, but as more people continued to arrive seeking employment houses were erected hurriedly in narrow streets with little regard to uniformity of design or elevation. There was no sewage system or piped water supply. Water was obtained from the town pump which was situated at the corner of Argyle Street and Market Street later the site of St. Paul's Church. There were also a number of wells notably one in Chester Street and the women carried the water on their heads in brightly polished tins.

By 1831 the population had risen to 2569, an increase in ten years of 2369 people and the need for a market, a police force and other essential amenities was urgent. In 1833 the First Improvement Act received the Royal Assent and by it, the affairs of Birkenhead plus Claughton, became the responsibility of the newly-appointed Commissioners. These consisted of the Mayor, two Bailiffs and four Aldermen of Liverpool plus sixty inhabitants of Birkenhead. The Act gave them the power to:— erect a market, light and cleanse the streets and maintain a separate police force. It also made the town responsible for maintaining its own roads and therefore relieved the Commissioners of contributions to the Highway and Turnpike rates. To provide the capital necessary for these, and other essential improvements, they were empowered to levy a rate of £8000.

The Commissioners set to work immediately. A sewerage system was commenced and the first Town Hall was erected in Hamilton

Street. It was a long low building which served as Civic Centre, Police Station, Courts, Bridewell, Registrar's Office and Fire Station. A police force was established consisting of one constable and three night watchmen whose duty hours were from 9 p.m. to 6 a.m. during which they were expected to light and clean the twenty street lamps. In those early days the policemen were also the firemen and in 1834 we find that the constable, during an outbreak of cholera, was further expected to lime-wash the houses of the poorer people in Back Chester Street.

Their first uniform consisted of a shiny top hat, blue swallow-tailed coat, blue trousers and cape. They were also provided with gloves and shoes plus a rattle, belt, lantern, stock and handcuffs. Since there was no Black Maria in those days, delinquents were handcuffed and hauled through the streets to the bridewell, so the constables needed to be sturdy individuals since beer was only $1^1/_2$d a pint and street brawls could be frequent and violent.

The Commissioners pursued their plans by erecting a market, adjacent to the Town Hall, which was completed within a year. It was partially covered and contained twenty-five shops and many stalls. The early residents who had arrived in Birkenhead before there were any shops and therefore had to cross the river to Liverpool to do their shopping, must have found the new market hall very convenient.

Building was continuing rapidly and the demand for houses was urgent to meet the needs of the growing population. Industry had come to the town. Another shipyard had been established at Wallasey Pool and between the two yards lay Thomas Brassey's busy lime and brick yard. There were chemical works on the northern bank of the Pool and in Tranmere a pier, graving dock and shipwright's yard were in operation.

William Laird's building plans had been delayed, but in 1833 one side of Hamilton Square was completed and new streets included Argyle Street, Bridge Street, Chester Street, Church Street, Waterloo Place, Ivy Street, Market Street, Cathcart Street and Grange Lane. The main streets followed Gillespie Graham's plan but in the southern part of the town the narrow streets and lack of planning was seen to have been an unfortunate mistake and the Commissioners drew up guidelines for future development.

About this time Francis Price, Lord of the Manor, wanted to sell the Woodside Ferry and he offered it to Hugh Williams, freehold for £250. Williams had leased it since 1823 and it was he who introduced steam ferries with the Etna in 1817. However he refused the offer considering the purchase would be a financial risk, but the ferry was

Oxton Health Centre, Balls Road. Formerly the site of the Spring Hill Water Works.

The Victorian Water Tower, Boundary Road.

badly managed and the service irregular and unsatisfactory so in 1835 the Woodside Ferry Company was formed by local business men who acquired the ferry and leased the Ferry Rights. The landing places were improved and the old boats replaced by bigger and better ones. An efficient and regular service was then established resulting in an increased number of passengers and the newly formed company prospered so much that by the end of the first year a group comprised of shareholders and some others, purchased the Ivy Rock Estate for another ferry and formed the Monks Ferry Company. About this time proposals had been made for the construction of a branch of the railway between Chester and Birkenhead which received official approval in 1837. By 1838 the Monks Ferry Hotel had been erected on the site of Ivy Rock and a steam ferry service established. It was proposed that the terminus for the new railway should be at Monks Ferry, but the Woodside Company brought legal action against the rival ferry claiming the ancient right of ferriage as lessees under Francis Price and they won their case. The Monks Ferry ceased to operate and the hotel, dock, pier and other assets of the company were sold to the railway.

The Woodside service must have been very regular since Henry Aspinall describes how a small bell was rung every half hour as a warning that the ferry boat was about to leave, but exceptions were sometimes made because he also tells us that his mother always shopped in Liverpool and there were times when he was sent ahead to say she would be down in a few minutes and would they detain the boat for her - which they did.

The early stage coaches of the late 18th century had coped with the number of passengers requiring transport at that time, but as the number of passengers using the ferry increased and from the early part of the 19th century the population of Birkenhead rose rapidly, so did the need for increased transport and the old Boathouse Inn became a busy coaching station. Henry Aspinall describes it as, "A small riverside inn with a fine old wooden veranda in front, painted green. Here people sat enjoying the fresh air and smoking their white clay church-warden pipes made at Brosely in Salop". In the 1830s the Innkeepers name was Poole and the inn became known as the Royal Mail Ferry Hotel, later in 1834 it was rebuilt and became the Woodside. As a coaching centre it had extensive stabling accomodation which existed until the end of the century.

The Royal Mail Coaches, painted dark blue, were always highly polished with coloured leather panels bearing the Royal Cipher. All coaches carried a coachman and a guard, but on the Royal Mail coaches they were dressed in scarlet with white hats and when they

The Town of Birkenhead – W. G. Herdman. Woodside and Monks Ferries 1846. (Courtesy Williamson Art Gallery).

entered or left a village or town the guards played favourite tunes of the day on the cornopean. For journeys at night they were always armed.

The four-horse stage coaches, drawn by teams of highly bred horses, were privately owned and were painted in bright colours, often yellow. A daily service, morning and afternoon, left Birkenhead for Chester and there was a similar service from the Black Horse Inn in Tranmere, while a further coach conveyed passengers from Tranmere to Parkgate whence they could continue their journey, on the Flint boat, to Wales. A daily service also left Rock Ferry for Shrewsbury and patrons from the Birkenhead Royal Mail Hotel were conveyed to Chester, Shrewsbury, Newton and Parkgate. Small two-horse vehicles also served the Wirral villages between Birkenhead and Chester, but the two special coaches, which ran in opposition, were the splendidly equipped Hirondelle and Hibernia. They often raced each other and were able to cover the 120 miles journey from Birkenhead to Cheltenham in twelve hours.

By 1840 a horse drawn bus service was introduced within the town to provide transport for business men to and from Woodside. Some years later when Hoylake began to attract new residents the only means of transport between there and Birkenhead was one of these old buses, the Atlas, which left the yard of the Woodside, by then Gough's Hotel, morning and afternoon.

The new town was in its infancy when Queen Victoria ascended the throne in 1837 and the townspeople in a demonstration of loyalty, celebrated her coronation by roasting an ox on the open ground near the first Town Hall.

Those early years were busy ones full of activity and about that time Thomas Brassey's lime and brick works were so profitable that he opened another yard at Tranmere Pool, placing his lime kilns along the river front. He used flat boats to bring the materials to Tranmere and to take the bricks he was supplying, for the new Custom's House, across the river to Liverpool, and using his business ability in another direction he constructed the New Chester Road from the Tranmere Hotel to Bromborough Village, with a fine macadamised surface throughout its four mile length. This road was needed to cope with increased coach traffic and was welcomed because it was a shorter route to Bromborough since vehicles had previously gone through Lower Tranmere, Bebington Village and Spital.

The building continued and within the next few years most of Hamilton Square was completed. Other elegant houses were erected in the streets adjacent to the square and in Chester Street and Argyle Street there were some fine shops, but there was no plumbing or gas. Eastwood, the first chemist, had his shop in Chester Street and sold many goods normally supplied by grocers and chandlers. We are told "....he did a roaring trade in candles and oil".

The need for street lighting had become urgent. W R S McIntyre tells us, "At night people became confused and lost in the miles of newly-laid-out streets. To go out after darkness had fallen was an adventure. Excavations, partially made roads and the chance of meeting with some ruffian on lonely stretches between the scattered building sites added danger to the discomfort of moving about the town in the evenings". So in 1840 William and John Somerville Jackson agreed to supply the town with gas. They built their gas works on a small peninsula which jutted out into Tranmere Pool and within the year the first gas lamps illuminated the streets. Since there were no gas mantles in those days the light came from the naked blue flame, but the lamps were a big improvement and were greatly appreciated. Subsequently, in 1858 the gas works were purchased by the Commissioners for the town and nearly a century later, in 1949, they became part of the North Western Gas Board.

With many rapidly developing building programmes the uncertain and inadequate supply of water posed a serious problem. Some houses had wells or pumps, others had no supply at all. At a public meeting called in 1841 to discuss the problem a resident of Church Street expressed himself thus, "I know perfectly well that the cry for water is great. In my own neighbourhood many of the inhabitants are at their wits' end what to do. Their landlord has promised them a well, but the water is unfit for use. I have dug a well for my stables, and I know many respectable families supply themselves from it".

Again it was William Jackson and his brother who agreed to solve the problem and in 1841 they formed a combined Gas and Water Company. Two years later Birkenhead's first Water Works were opened at Spring Hill in Balls Road. When in 1858 the Commisioners purchased the Company, the town therefore acquired both Gas and Water Works. Shortly afterwards, a further supply became available when the new Water Works were opened at Flaybrick and since these were situated 173 feet above sea level they could supply the higher parts of town, but the problem was not solved even though there were eventually three more pumping stations, one in Prenton one in Tranmere and another at Ford, making a total of five altogether.

The problem continued into the next century because the demand always exceeded the supply so that in 1911, the Corporation embarked on a major project and purchased a large area of land in North Wales which included the Alwen Valley. The plan proposed was known as a Gravitation Scheme in which there were no wells or pumping machinery. From the Alwen Reservoir, which they constructed, the water would flow through cast iron and steel pipes to Birkenhead finding its own natural level on its way and as a further precaution, in case of emergency, a reservoir holding 31,000,000 gallons was built at Thingwall. On the 15th August 1921 the chairman of the Water Committee opened a tap on the balcony of the Town Hall and the Alwen Gravitation Scheme became operational. Since then Birkenhead has enjoyed a plentiful and adequate water supply.

4

New Ventures

From 1842-46 William Jackson was Chairman of the Commissioners and during his period of leadership a number of major projects were undertaken. The first was the provision of a park. This was an unusual and imaginative venture since it was the first municipal or public park in the country and therefore became the forerunner of a movement then unknown, but now readily accepted to provide at public expense, open spaces for recreation in large towns.

In 1843, having obtained the necessary Parliamentary authority, some 226 acres of land were purchased. Of these 125 acres were for public use while the remaining 101 were scheduled to be sold for plots, the profits from which, it was hoped, would offset the building expenses incurred in creating the park. The land purchased was poor. It was common land, low lying and marshy and had been known in the 17th century as the Lowerfields, but it provided good cover for foxes and there was even a small farm kept by a Mrs. Hannah Mutch.

William Jackson approached Joseph Paxton, Head Gardener to the Duke of Devonshire at Chatsworth House, inviting him to submit plans for the park, but when they visited the area together and Joseph Paxton realised the poor quality of the land, he doubted the feasibility of the work he was invited to undertake but fortunately for Birkenhead, he had second thoughts and accepted the assignment as a personal challenge.

The first turf was cut in 1844 and for about three years 1000 men were employed in transforming this unpromising area of land into a place of great beauty. Paxton's design was informal and natural. The marshes were drained and as the soil was removed to form the lakes it was used to make rounded hillocks giving a variety of levels and providing shelter from the prevailing winds for many of the plants and shrubs.

Edward Kemp supervised the laying out of the park to Paxton's design. A carriage drive was constructed round the perimeter and winding paths made around the lakes and between the plantations. Of the many attractive features some of the most outstanding were the lakes with their population of swans, ducks and other water fowl, the Swiss Bridge and the Boathouse-cum-Bandstand.

A design for an imposing main entrance was submitted to the Commissioners by Lewis Hornblower, a young Liverpool architect who had been engaged to supervise the erection of the various lodges according to Paxton's plan. Paxton however thought it too ornate and it was only after some modification that it was finally approved and the main entrance, incorporating two lodges, was erected. There were six other lodges situated by the main gates and of these, the Italian Lodge, Park Road South and the Central Lodge, Ashville Road, are considered to be the most pleasing in architectural detail and design.

In 1845 Edward Kemp was appointed Park Superintendent and by 1846 the park was almost finished, but the official opening was delayed until the following year to coincide with the opening of the docks.

As time passed, a number of houses of good quality were built on the perimeter, but never as many as Paxton had envisaged and the Commissioners had hoped for. A change in the use of the park, which came with time, was the introduction of various recreations, cricket, football, archery, quoits, fishing and curling in winter. With changing interests some of these pastimes have been dropped. We still have cricket, football and fishing, but today's sports include bowls, tennis, jogging, sponsored walks and cycling events.

No account of the Park would be complete without recalling the visit in 1850 of the American, Frederick Law Olmsted. Birkenhead's park made a lasting impression on him and when, some years later, he was commissioned to design Central Park, New York, he based many of his ideas on Paxton's plan. With nearly 700 acres at his disposal he was able to expand on the ideas he had so admired and in subsequent visits to England he always endeavoured to visit Birkenhead, the source of his inspiration.

By the 1840s the number of ships using the port of Liverpool had steadily increased to the point where the existing docks were inadequate. The tonnage of these sailing ships was not great, about 500 tons, but there were many of them and as the century advanced, the tall ships, the four masted barques and the clipper types carrying 1000 to 3000, tons arrived. Delay in discharging and loading cargoes was inevitable and there were complaints from the merchants and also from the seamen who had to anchor in the river waiting for vacant berths.

Wallasey Pool had long been considered suitable for dock

construction, but early tentative plans had been abandoned. So, in the summer of 1843, realising the advantages to Birkenhead of docking facilities, William Jackson, John Laird, William Potter and others bought large areas of land at Wallasey Pool and engaged an engineer to prepare plans for a suitable development. They did not disclose their scheme until they presented it to the Commissioners at their meeting on 7th November. All the preliminary work was done, the land purchased and the necessary surveys completed. If the Commissioners were in favour they could apply without loss of time to Parliament for authority to proceed. They were in favour and eventually, after much Parliamentary delay and discussion, the Royal Assent was given in July 1844 and on Wednesday 23rd October Sir Philip Egerton laid the foundation stone of the Birkenhead docks. This was such an important day for the town that a general holiday was declared. The streets were decorated, bells pealed, guns were fired and crowded ferry boats brought many sightseers from Liverpool. After the ceremony there were banquets and dinners plus beef and bread for the poorer people and the celebrations ended with a grand display of fireworks in Argyle Street.

Work on the first two docks proceeded rapidly employing about 1000 labourers and since there were an equal number being employed on the Park at the same time, there was a serious housing shortage. To accomodate the workers on the docks, blocks of flats, the Dock Cottages, were erected at the north end of the town. The architect for these was C. E. Lang and they were built by Hugh Williams. His father, also Hugh Williams, had been a joiner and builder and having built many houses and shops had built the Pier Hotel for himself. Although Hugh junior had leased the Ferry from Francis Price for many years, he had refused to buy it when it was offered to him and subsequently followed his father into the building trade.

In 1843 Birket Hall was demolished and the gardens laid out in streets. The Price family had not lived there for many years and a succession of tenants had used it for different purposes. About the 1820s it became a boarding school for young ladies run by the Misses Koster and some excitement was caused locally when one of the young ladies eloped.

William Jackson purchased Francis Price's remaining property in Birkenhead, including Saint Mary's, in 1844, and thus became Lord of the Manor of Claughton. Choosing an elevated site in Egerton Road, he erected a new Manor House, Claughton Hall, built in Storeton stone with an elegant and richly decorated interior and surrounded by beautiful gardens designed by Joseph Paxton.

The new Lord of the Manor followed a trend for residents to move inland from the riverside as the approaches to the Ferry became crowded with streets of smaller houses and shops and the value of the original elegant villas depreciated. Hilda Gamlin tells us, "...the owners of two good houses near the river, alive to the disadvantages of their position removed them to surroundings befitting their style which would prove more remunerative. The stones were dissected and re-erected in Park Road South". The houses are now 90 and 92. Built of Storeton stone they stand by the park gates and were recently converted into small flats for pensioners.

With its elevated position proving an advantage Claughton became a favourite residential area and fine houses were erected. They were surrounded by open fields with pleasing views across the new park down to the river and it was about this time that the old Grange Farm was absorbed into urban development. Another acceptable area for more affluent residents was Clifton Park situated on the slopes of Tranmere Hill and also surrounded by open fields. It was, as the name suggests, developed as a private residential park containing a number of well spaced houses and a pleasing rural feature was the small stream which flowed through it to join the Rubicon at the foot of the hill.

Situated off Conway Street was another similar development laid out in 1835. Mortimer describes it thus, "A small enclosure called Parkfield deserves particular notice. It contains several villas in a very good style, surrounded with pleasure grounds, forming a little park of about fifteen acres". Mrs. Hilda Gamlin, author of some delightful books on Birkenhead and Wirral, was one of the residents there living in "Camden Lawn". Streets of less expensive houses were also being built at a rapid rate and it was said that 500 new homes appeared in 1844.

During this boom period of private building the Commissioners were also actively engaged on a number of important public works. At the time that land was purchased for the park a large area was also acquired at Flaybrick Hill for a Public Cemetery and Joseph Paxton was asked to submit designs for it. This project was unfortunately delayed for some years and it was not until 1861 that Edward Kemp, using his own designs, was commissioned to complete the work envisaged by Paxton.

Other projects were quickly completed and in 1845 a new Market Hall was opened. The first building had proved totally inadequate to the needs of the town so the new one was planned on a much larger scale. It was built of stone with a wrought iron roof supported by

The Main Entrance, Birkenhead Park.

The Central Lodge, Birkenhead Park.

columns connected by arched cast-iron girders and was lofty and airy with a generous floor space of 430 feet by 131 feet. The main entrance was in Oliver Street, later Market Place South, and was approached by a flight of wide stone steps. Ninety-two elegant globe lamps lighted the interior and the central avenue featured two attractive fountains. The hall accomodated forty-two shops and seventy-six stalls with the addition of a number of tables for horticultural produce. It was described at the time as a pleasant rendezvous where the fountains cast a refreshing spray. In 1974 the building, once thought to be fireproof, was badly damaged by fire, but it continued in use until 1977 when the new market was opened in Grange Shopping Precinct.

Much needed abattoirs were also built in 1845. These were situated near the mouth of Tranmere Pool so that the movement of cattle interfered as little as possible with life in the township and since a high standard of development was required they were well built with excellent facilities for hygiene, following plans prepared by Mr. Brine, the town's surveyor. Shortly afterwards a tannery was established nearby, but the glue works, using waste material from the tannery, were not built until some thirty years later.

The beach at Woodside with its hard dry sand, attractive setting, bathing machines and donkeys had become a favourite venue for bathing, attracting not only local residents, but visitors from Liverpool and the surrounding countryside. There was understandable dismay, therefore, when the effluent from these two new undertakings began to foul the river at the Tranmere end of the beach and this was one of the first causes of the polution which eventually became so severe that it killed all marine life in the Mersey.

The Police Force established in 1833 soon proved inadequate and by 1839 had been increased to one Parish Constable, two Day Constables and five Night Watchmen. The town had also acquired a fire engine. Yet further increases were necessary during these years of rapid change. The first Police Surgeon was appointed in 1844 and by the next year the Force numbered forty-five, a Superintendent, four Inspectors and forty Constables. The law was strictly enforced and penalties for even minor offences were severe.

When the original plans to introduce a railway line between Birkenhead and Chester had to be abandoned they were postponed, not forgotton, and eventually after much discussion and counter-discussion the first railway cuttings were begun in 1838. About that time the Woodside Ferry Company had run into financial difficulties. Fares had been reduced and the resulting loss of profits forced the Company to sell out to the Railway.

The new line to Chester was opened in 1840 with its terminus in Grange Lane, close to what was later the site of Town Station and the route passed through Bebington, Hooton, Sutton and Mollington. The Railway Company then owned both ferries and announced their intention of discontinuing annual contracts. Birkenhead's commuters protested strongly since this meant added expense for them and the outcome was that William Jackson purchased the Woodside Ferry and immediately re-sold it to the Birkenhead Commissioners.

The introduction of the railway brought many benefits to the town and so in September 1843 the Commissioners purchased the Monks Ferry Estate from the Railway Company and in 1844 a tunnel was constructed between Grange Lane Station and Monks Ferry enabling trains to convey passengers to the river front. The Monks Ferry was re-opened and Mortimer describing the new service in 1845 tells us. "At present the departure of the packets from this ferry is regulated by the railway trains, of which there are eleven daily, and as the boats take casual passengers also, the additional accomodation afforded by them is very great; the landing at the pier is excellent, and the packets are worked with as much regularity as their connection with the trains will admit".

Shortly afterwards the railway was further extended from Grange Lane to the docks, its route unfortunately, cutting across the well-planned system of streets. Writing a century later Sir Charles Reilly offered the following criticism. "Dock construction necessitated the connection of the docks with the railway to Chester . . . the line running parallel to the lower course of Bridge End Brook and cutting across the rectangular grid of streets already built and leaving awkward triangular patches difficult to utilize. These are now builders yards and dumps. The ruthless cutting of a diagonal railway across the formal plan of rectangular streets by destroying the meaning of the latter, helped to degrade the area.

The close proximity of Monks Ferry to the Chester Street shops and the attractive new market brought increased trade to this part of the town and about 1845 John Somerville Jackson erected the imposing block of shops-cum-houses called the Market Cross. These were planned by a local architect, Walter Scott, and built in polished Storeton stone with well designed richly decorated exteriors. As well as providing accomodation for quality shops they were considered to be a major undertaking in the town, equal in architectural importance to Hamilton Square and, therefore, a desirable visual asset.

As important building works progressed within the town major alterations were made to the landing place at Woodside Ferry. A report of 1843 estimated that some two million passengers used the ferry annually and the improvements were designed to afford greater protection for passengers in adverse weather conditions. A high wall, twenty feet wide, was constructed down the centre of the existing wide slipway so that it formed a pier jutting out into the river and acting as a breakwater to the slipways on either side. Ferry boats were therefore able to choose the more sheltered berth. The two largest and quickest boats sailing from Woodside were iron vessels from Laird's Yard, the Prince and the Queen while the smaller boats in service were named Nun, Eliza Price, Kingfisher, Cleveland and Lord Morpeth. The pier, bounded by a stone ballustrade, was illuminated by gas lamps and at the end stood a small lighthouse and a large bell which was used as a fog warning. It became a pleasant custom for ladies to take afternoon strolls along the pier from which vantage point they could watch the passengers as they walked along the sloping slipways to and from the pay gates which were situated near Gough's Woodside Hotel.

The ferry service operated from five in the morning until midnight, leaving Liverpool and Woodside every half hour, but with new boats building the only obstacle to a more frequent service was considered to be, ". . . the shamefully neglected state of the Liverpool landing places".

Since the 1830s and 1840s were years of ceaseless building it is not surprising that many of the town's churches were built during that period to meet the needs of the growing population. True, some were raised by public subscription, but others were generously donated by leading members of the community. St. Mary's did not remain the only church and school for very long. In less than twenty years ten others were built, their spires and towers becoming prominent features of the skyline and their sites indicating the general movement of the population away from the southern part of the headland.

The Wesleyan Methodist Chapel was built in 1830 by public subscription and stood in Price Street near Hamilton Square. It was a brick building with a stone front and portico and provided schoolrooms where the older children paid what was considered to be a high fee of four pence per week.

Saint Werburgh's built in 1834 was the first Catholic Church in the town and was built in Grange Lane within sight of St. Mary's. It is a stone building and originally, as well as an adjacent presbytery, there were two schools, capable of taking 600 children, plus a house for the schoolmaster. It is now the only surviving church in the shopping centre and still retains its old burial ground.

Holy Trinity Church was situated in Price Street, also near Hamilton Square. Built in 1837 of white stone it had a tower eighty-eight feet high and the grotesque gargoyles which surrounded the belfry were a prominent and well known feature. The Reverend Joseph Baylee was the first incumbent. He was a tireless pastor and justly renowned personality and was the founder of St. Aidan's Theological College which stood, until recent years, in Shrewsbury Road.

An Independent Chapel was erected in 1839 in Argyle Street at the junction with Cleveland Street. Architecturally it blended well with the buildings in Hamilton Square, but in recent years its usefulness past, it was replaced by an office building.

The Scots Kirk built in 1844, to meet the needs of the increasing Scottish population, stood in Conway Street and was built by public subscription. It was described as a handsome building with an adjacent burial ground, and since the area at the front was laid out with plants and flowers, presented a very pleasing appearance. Schools were also provided where the standard of education was reputedly high but the fees were very low. Its site is now part of the car park by the Asda Supermarket.

St. John's Church stood near St. Werburgh's in Grange Lane from 1845. With an exeptionally tall, graceful steeple, the exterior was in red stone and unlike most churches, it stood in a north south direction. It was erected and endowed at the expense of John Somerville Jackson, his brother William Jackson and Joseph Mallaby. Schools with accommodation for 450 children were provided nearby and funded from other sources. Both church and schools have given way to modern development, but their memory is perpetuated in the names St. John's Street and St. John's Pavement.

A Welsh Independent Chapel, described as a fine building, was erected in Oliver Street in 1846, but it too has gone with the passage of time.

St. Anne's Church was built in Beckwith Street in 1847 at the sole expense of William Potter. It is an elegant building, in red sandstone from the Claughton Quarries, with a lofty spire and still serves the community. William Potter, again at his own expense, provided a Free School for 500 children, near the church. In recent years the school has merged with another in more modern premises.

Christchurch was also erected at the sole expense of William Potter in 1847. It stands at the junction of Bessborough Road and Christchurch Road, has an octagonal spire and like St. Anne's, was also built with red sandstone from the Claughton Firs Quarry nearby. The extensive crypts were designed for schools capable of providing for 760 children. The Church still retains its schools, but in modern purpose built accommodation.

St. James' Church, with its tall spire, is a notable landmark and stands at the north end of the town at the junction of seven roads. It was dedicated to St. James, one of the patrons of the Priory, and was founded and erected in 1847 by William Potter, William Jackson, John, McGregor and William Laird. The stone used came from the quarries at Flaybrick Hill. When a school for 500 children was built nearby, on land given by the Birkenhead Dock Company, the major cost was borne by the same group of philanthropists who provided the Church. The school was closed in the early 1930s.

The census returns for 1841 had shown a population of 8223, an increase in ten years of nearly 6,000. There were 3787 males, 2009 over twenty-one and 1178 under twenty-one, while females numbered 4436 with 2473 over twenty-one and 1963 under twenty-one. Houses were listed as 1270 inhabited, 91 uninhabited plus 119 under construction. Yet the rate of building could scarcely keep pace with the influx of new residents for by 1851 the population reached an amazing 24,285.

An article in Chambers' Edinburgh Journal, 17th May 1845, made the following observations, "One of the facts which have most deeply impressed us lately is the sudden rise of a new city in England. A city we are accustomed to consider as the growth of centuries, for cities have heretofore always taken centuries to build. But now, such is the hugeness of the power created by the industry and wealth of this country, there is at least one city which will undoubtedly have risen within the brief space between the boyhood and manhood of its first inhabitants. We allude to Birkenhead on the Mersey, near Liverpool".

Birkenhead became not a city, but the largest town in Cheshire and a busy port. By the 1840s thousands had already settled here and thousands more followed, but where did they come from and why?

During the Middle Ages the Black Death, or Bubonic Plague, with other infectious diseases caused many deaths throughout the country. It is estimated that the population of England was probably halved in the years between 1300 and 1500, but by the 16th century it was steadily rising again. At the same time changes were being made in farming practices. With the deaths of their owners many small farms became vacant, and the ready availability of land enabled other farms to become bigger, and since the ancient system of cultivating common land in strips was wasteful, it gradually came to an end and both fields and common land were enclosed.

A farm labourer worked long hours for very small wages and since these were paid on a daily basis, when the weather was unsuitable for work, his wages were nil. However, by cultivating his share of common land and using the common grazing land it had always been possible for him to produce his own food. The enclosure of land denied him this and since the large farms tended to employ seasonal labour the degree of poverty, among the lower paid, became acute in many agricultural regions.

Cottage industries had always helped to provide extra income in rural areas and the goods produced in this way were many and varied. For instance, in sheep rearing areas whole families would be engaged in carding, spinning and weaving, but the factories of the Industrial Revolution produced cloth more cheaply and the cottage-based industries largely disappeared.

The Corn Laws had been enforced from the 15th century onwards to protect the farmer, but by keeping the price of corn high they also put up the price of bread and this was another factor which caused great hardship to the lower paid workers. Such conditions of poverty had already, over the years, caused a drift away from the rural areas to the factories of the industrial towns and Birkenhead offered both work and opportunity in a new town which still presented an attractive, semi-rural appearance.

In Ireland the soil, climate and many smallholdings favoured livestock farming and to offset the price of corn the Irish farmers planted potatoes which became a staple part of their diet. In 1845 and 1846 potato blight ruined the crops and caused famine. It is estimated that by 1851 a million people had died and over one-and-a-half million had emigrated. Many of these emigrants, en-route to New York via Liverpool, never progressed beyond the Mersey. Birkenhead offered work and food and they stayed.

Scotland and Wales were both countries of limited opportunity which also contributed new residents to the town, so that eventually the population represented all parts of the United Kingdom.

Coming from widely different parts of the country to a town without traditional customs, the new residents brought their own folklore with them. Easter was the time for Egg Pacing when hard boiled eggs with brightly-dyed shells were taken to the Park and

Nos. 90 and 92 Park Road South. Two of the first houses built in the town and removed in the 1840s from their original site on the river front.

rolled down the hillocks. Hilda Gamlin describing this custom wrote, "To these hillocks children would bring baskets of Pace Eggs on Easter Monday. Wickets were fixed at intervals at the foot of the 'bonks' when the children took their eggs to the top of the hills and rolled them down, aiming to pass them unbroken between the wickets. Prizes were offered for the two youngsters who displayed the most skill in the rolling and for the ones who brought the largest assortment of decorated eggs... Large crowds of children and adults watched. It was followed by an Easter Day Dance performed by the youngsters who were then given buns to eat". Although this custom has generally died out children have been seen, in recent years, rolling eggs down the hillocks in Ashville Road at Easter time.

The first of May became a day for merry-making. A miniature carnival used to assemble in Abbey Street composed of men dressed as women. The May Queen was always a man wearing a dress decorated with bright flowers and ribbons and a ridiculous floral and beribboned headdress. The somewhat boisterous procession danced along accompanied by a band composed of tin whistles, a kettle drum, little rattles and small trays used as tambourines. Their route lay along Chester Street, past the old ferry pay gates, past Gough's (the Woodside) Hotel and into Hamilton Street from where they reached the green fields which are now Hinson Street. The Maypole was erected there and the women dancers, dressed in pretty costumes, joined the men and the whole company danced round the Maypole.

In the 1840s Tranmere was a separate village with its own long established traditions. One of these also concerned May Day, when the young people from the village gathered may blossom or hawthorn in the Rubicon Valley and hung the branches over the doorways of the houses.

Until motor lorries replaced the horse drawn ones there was a procession throughout the town every year during the month of May of the 'May Horses'. These were the shire horses carefully groomed, with shining horse brasses and harnesses decorated with flowers. They made a brave and colourful sight and prizes were awarded for the best turn-outs.

A reminder of the old May Day festivities continued until recent years when children formed small processions depicting a bride and her attendants. As they roamed the streets they cried, "Penny for the May Queen".

It is not really surprising that customs such as these and others, relics of a rural past and often with centuries old pagan origins, have died out and are now forgotten by the present day descendants of the early residents of the new town on the headland.

By 1847 the first two docks, the Egerton and the Morpeth were completed. The park had been finished and opened to the public for some months, but its official opening was delayed to enable a joint ceremony to take place.

Easter Monday, 5th April 1847, dawned bright and fair and the townspeople enjoyed a public holiday with the added benefit of a half day's pay for many of the workers through the generosity of their employers. The streets were decked with flags, bands played and many visitors crossed the river to join the crowds on the banks of Wallasey Pool and share the general excitement.

At noon Viscount Morpeth, Chief Commissioner of Woods and Ferries, performed the first opening ceremony by sailing from Monks Ferry on the paddle-boat Lord Warden, recently built at Laird's yard, past Woodside and through the entrance to the new docks. After disembarking the official party and their guests proceeded to one of the new warehouses where they enjoyed a banquet, or 'breakfast', which, with the toasts and speeches, lasted all afternoon. Later that day a ship from Patagonia sailed into the docks and discharged a cargo of guano. Birkenhead docks were operational.

At five o'clock Lord Morpeth drove to the Park where, after the speeches were made, he planted a tree. Thousands had thronged to the Park, and Conway Street was lined with vendors of all kinds. Although the afternoon became showery, the general enthusiasm was not dampened. The bands paraded in the Park and a group of Lancashire Bell Ringers added to the gaiety by playing in the bandstand over the boathouse, but the rural sports were the main feature of the afternoon. An old handbill shows their variety and the prizes offered.

The general celebrations ended with a fine display of fireworks, but for the Commissioners and their guests there was a grand ball, also held in the suitably decorated warehouse. The Liverpool Mercury commenting on the celebrations reported, "During the evening the greatest hilarity and enjoyment prevailed; each and every one seemed determined that the beginning of a new era in the history of Birkenhead should not pass over without some enjoyment."

Birkenhead with its new park and many open spaces between the houses had become a pleasant town and attracted many visitors, principally from Liverpool. They came to stroll through the wide streets towards the Park and, since this was some distance from the Ferry, benches were conveniently placed at intervals along Conway Street. Also, at no great distance from Monks Ferry and the railway station in Grange Lane lay another attraction in the pretty wooded valley of the Rubicon, a popular area of great natural beauty. The stretch of the river where it widened before flowing into Tranmere Pool became known as the Happy Valley and Hilda Gamlin described it as a lovely vale where wild flowers grew in season, primroses, wild violets, woodbine, honeysuckle and wild roses. There were many thistles which attracted butterflies and in the Autumn the brambles provided blackberries. No wonder Gypsies sometimes pitched their tents there. A further attraction was the popular pastime of boating on Tranmere Pool where the building of the embankment had created a natural lake.

Easter 1847 had seen the successful opening of the first docks and the Park. The future success and prosperity of the town seemed assured, but by the end of the year there were financial difficulties. Constructing the docks had proved to be more expensive than was anticipated and the Dock Company was getting short of funds. At the same time there was the great railway crash which caused such a financial crisis in Liverpool that the banks were closed for several weeks.

All work on the docks ceased. Many people left the town and there was great depression, distress and disappointment in Birkenhead. Building ceased and houses were left unfinished, while grass grew in the streets. It is recorded that, "... Price Street grew a notable crop of dog daisies, and its sole occupants were donkeys grazing, and geese".

The image of the town changed rapidly. Instead of being called the city of the future it was renamed the city of the dead.

5

Financial Recovery and Progress

The Birkenhead Commissioners were determined to revive the prosperity of the town despite the financial collapse of 1847 and since the first residents had seen the original small hamlet as a desirable residential area they decided to promote this image. Rents were reduced and Joseph Craven, an estate agent actively interested in the development of the town, proposed a reduction in the fares on the ferries from two pence to one penny. These measures meant that more people came to live in the town and an annual loss on the ferries was changed to a considerable profit. Careful administration was necessary, but as the Commissioners had hoped, the fortunes of the town gradually improved.

From 1824, when William Laird opened the Birkenhead Iron Works at Wallasey Pool, the firm had prospered. John Laird joined his father in 1828, the year in which they built their first iron ship. They also built wooden ships when required, but maintained their faith in iron ships, despite opposition, and by 1840 they had gained an international reputation and had exported their iron vessels to many parts of the world.

The Admiralty had always been opposed to iron ships, but in 1843 Laird's were given the contract for a frigate to be called Vulcan. The name was later changed to Birkenhead and she was launched in 1845, but a year later was converted to a troopship.

On 26th February 1852 she struck a rock and sank with the loss of 454 soldiers who gave their lives to save the women and children on board and maintained disciplined lines on deck while the ship went down. Their heroism is recorded in Birkenhead by a picture which hangs in the Williamson Art Gallery.

The financial crisis of the 1840s had also affected the shipyard and the situation was so severe that many people assumed the firm had failed, but by 1850 a new era of prosperity began. Restrictions on cargoes were removed and ship owners began to change to the new iron vessels. Although work on the docks was suspended ships had continued to use the Egerton and Morpeth Docks and in 1857 an Act of Parliament brought the docks on both sides of the river under the management of the newly formed Mersey Docks and Harbour Board and John Laird was a member of the Board. The Morpeth Dock was enlarged and work continued steadily to enlarge, improve and complete the dock system, but as the work progressed Wallasey Pool became unsuitable for Laird's and so in 1856 the Yard was transferred to the river front between Monk's Ferry and Birkenhead Ferry.

As the affairs of the town became financially stable again the Commissioners sought to extend the amenities available and so in 1856 they decided to establish a public library and Birkenhead became the first unincorporated Borough to take advantage of the Public Libraries Act of 1850. The library was in Price Street and opened with a stock of 3,132 volumes and was so popular that within a year larger premises were necessary and therefore it was moved to rooms over the newly erected Post Office in Conway Street. By 1864 a further move was required and it was then housed in a purpose built building in Hamilton Street.

There was also a great need for public transport within the town. A horse drawn bus had operated from about 1840, but its main purpose was to convey business men to and from Woodside. When therefore George Francis Train, from Boston U.S.A., came to Birkenhead in 1859 with his idea for a street railway the Commissioners were readily interested, although other towns had rejected the idea and, influenced by John Laird, they agreed to his proposals. Thus Birkenhead became the first town in Europe to adopt street railways and the system came into operation on 30th August 1860, the original route being from Woodside to the Park. The trams were an instant success and a press report of the time tells us, ". . . carriages of the street railway, each drawn by two magnificent horses, commenced running from 10 o'clock and during the whole of the day they were filled as rapidly as possible." Although the fare was six pence, 4,360 passengers were carried on the first day and visitors came to the town to see Birkenhead's new and wonderful form of transport. George Francis Train was so elated by his success that he gave a magnificent banquet to celebrate and invited all the crowned heads of Europe, the Pope and Garibaldi to attend, but these notable guests failed to grace his table.

1861 saw a milestone in the history of the town when with Claughton, Oxton, Tranmere and part of Bebington it attained the status of a Parliamentary Borough and elections were held for the first Member of Parliament. There were two candidates Thomas Brassey Jnr. and John Laird. John Laird was duly elected. He retired from the Yard and as its M.P. served Birkenhead faithfully for many years. To mark his election he built the Borough Hospital on land in

Park Road North, generously donated by Thomas Brassey. The foundation stone was laid in 1862 and the building opened in 1864. There were four wards, three male and one female and the new hospital provided much needed care for the sick of the town. With the opening of the new Arrowe Park Hospital the building became redundant and was demolished.

In 1858, shortly before John Laird retired from the Yard, Laird's launched a paddle boat which caused the Illustrated London News to observe, "There are some peculiarities about her construction which are worth notice. The hull and boilers are built of steel plates." Laird's had scored a notable success in producing the first steel ship. It was built for Dr. David Livingstone, the Scottish missionary and explorer, and was designed for use on the Zambesi River, where it was called the Ma Robert. Livingstone who was sailing to Africa from Liverpool, in the larger vessel Pearl, came to Birkenhead to personally supervise the stowing of his new ship and stores aboard her and during his visit here he stayed with John Laird in Hamilton Square. A street named after him commemorates the visit.

In the summer of 1862 a mystery ship was launched by Laird's. It bore no name and was known only as the 290, and although the hull was pierced for guns there were no guns aboard. After taking on a great quantity of coal the 290 left the river apparently to undergo her sea trials, but she never returned. She reached the Azores where guns were taken on board and there was named the Alabama. The mystery ship was, of course, the Confederate warship which caused so much damage during the American Civil War. It is said that during her two years at sea she sank 55 merchant ships and one Naval vessel. After the war was over the U.S.A. claimed compensation for the loss of shipping inflicted by British built Confederate cruisers, of which the Alabama was the most famous. An international tribunal found the claim proven and in 1870 the British Government was forced to pay three million pounds in damages.

The Alabama had caused great interest and speculation locally, but two years later another vessel literally shook the residents of Birkenhead and Liverpool with shattering results. The Lottie Sleigh was a small ship lying at anchor off Woodside on the night of 15th January 1864. She was bound for Africa and her cargo included ten tons of dynamite. A fire, accidentally started on board when a lamp was dropped, spread rapidly and the crew abandoned ship. The enormous explosion which followed caused widespread damage to houses near the river in Birkenhead and Liverpool and local glaziers quickly exhausted their stocks of glass. Fortunately no lives were lost, but the ship was blown to fragments the only surviving parts

The statue of John Laird, Hamilton Square.

being the figure-head which now belongs to the Royal Insurance Company, and is on permanent loan to the Liverpool Maritime Museum, and a deadeye and shackle which was thrown over half a mile and landed in Saint Mary's churchyard. This is now displayed in the Williamson Art Gallery.

In 1861 when Birkenhead became a Parliamentary Borough the population was 35,929, but with the inclusion of Tranmere, Claughton and Oxton the total population of the new Borough was 50,101. After the financial crisis of the late 1840s the Commissioners had managed the town's affairs skilfully and debts had been paid off, but with the extended boundaries, revenues were increased and it became possible to consider major improvements within the town.

Woodside Ferry continued to carry an ever increasing number of passengers so in 1861 a new floating landing stage with a connecting bridge was moored to the river wall, adjacent to the old pier with its small lighthouse. New ferry boats began to come into service by 1864, first the Cheshire and later the Lancashire and the Woodside. These were the first boats with bright airy saloons on their main decks. The ferry approaches were also improved and since similar work had been carried out on the Liverpool landing stage passengers travelled in much greater comfort.

The Improvement Act of 1863 gave an outline of the Commissioners' future plans. By it they were authorised to erect a Town Hall, Public Baths and Police Stations. Further projects included widening Grange Lane and the making of a new road, Borough Road, between Whetstone Lane and Hamilton Street. Not all these plans were developed immediately. The site for the new Town Hall had been reserved for some thirty years, but the townspeople had to wait another twenty years before the foundation stone was laid in 1883.

Grange Lane and the new Borough Road were priorities and by 1870 work on Borough Road was almost complete. The River Rubicon, crossed at intervals by rustic bridges with handrails, and flowing through its pretty wooded valley, disappeared and with it the natural division between Birkenhead and Tranmere. Views expressed by contemporary writers suggest that the loss of this natural beauty spot caused some regret locally, although the district close to Whetstone Lane being known as the Woodlands still reminds us of the Happy Valley.

By 1870 Tranmere Pool had almost virtually disappeared. The building of the embankment had restricted the natural flow of tidal water and when in 1840 the Gas Works were established, on the peninsula in the Pool, the steady outflow of refuse from them polluted the water which was soon reduced to a sluggish stream. Eventually as the Gas Works needed to be extended, to provide for the ever growing town, the land was reclaimed for this purpose and was also used for wood yards and other commercial enterprises.

The new Mersey Docks and Harbour Board, after extending the Morpeth Dock continued to expand the system. A graving dock had been built and water let into the Great Float by 1860 and in 1866 the Alfred Dock and the Northern entrances were opened, with some ceremony, by the Duke of Edinburgh, a son of Queen Victoria. Shortly afterwards the Vittoria Dock was constructed and in 1868 corn warehouses were built on the East Float. Although the corn was at first sent inland for milling, with the later building of the flour mills, Birkenhead was to become a large and important milling centre.

Private building continued. The tram lines were soon extended along Park Roads East and South and continued up Palm Grove where the horses were stabled. Claughton and Oxton, therefore, continued to be favourite residential districts and many substantial houses were erected. Yet building did not follow a continuous pattern and there were many spaces between the sites. Harry Neilson describes the house in Westbourne Road, in which he was born in 1861, as being surrounded by fields. He also mentions the Queens Hotel in Park Road East and the small thatched cottages dotted here and there near it, for which the owners claimed squatters rights. In 1863 his parents moved to a new house, "Airliewood", in what is now Forest Road, but was then an area of forest land, mostly Scotch Firs, part of which had to be cleared to make way for the house. On the opposite side of the road stood the Manor House or Claughton Farm.

With the increase in housing more churches were erected. In 1851 the first Saint Saviour's was built in Oxton, followed in 1854 by Our Lady's in Price Street and by Saint Paul's, Lower Tranmere, in 1855. 1864 saw the first Saint Laurence's in Park Street and all these churches provided schools.

The care of the poor and destitute who came to the town, from its earliest years, had always posed a problem and when in 1861 Birkenhead elected its own Board of Guardians they immediately built the Tranmere Workhouse which was completed in 1863. It provided food and shelter, but the conditions were spartan. Aware of its deficiencies the Board made many improvements in ensuing years and by 1913 new wards provided 322 beds and the building became

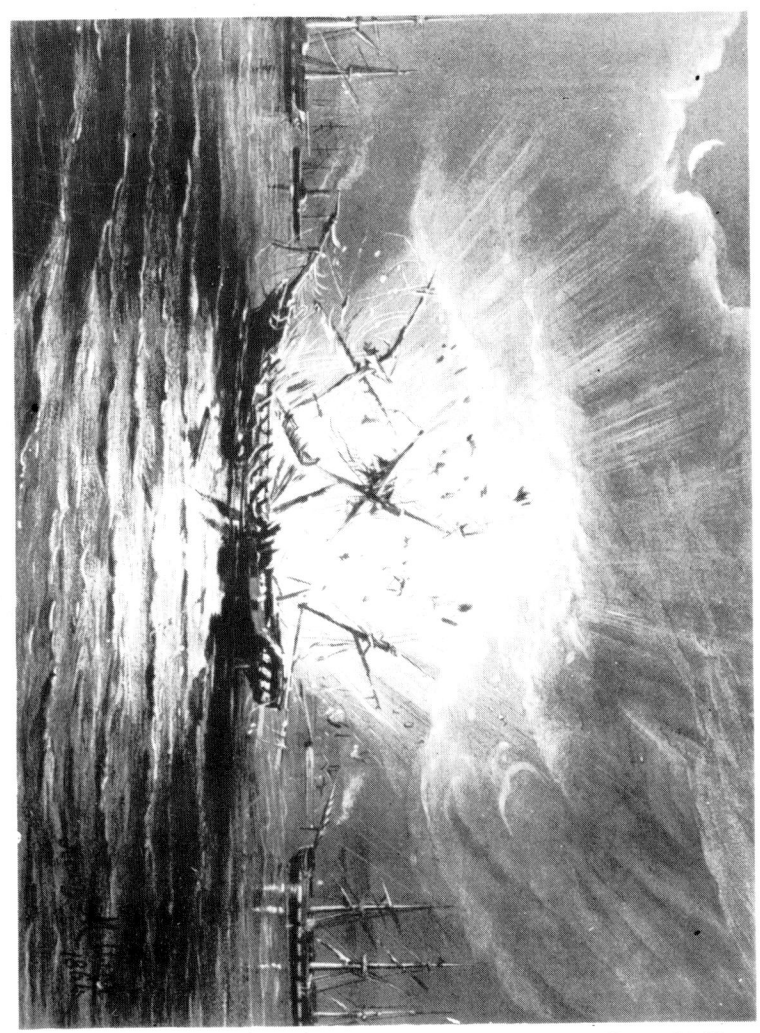

The explosion on the Lottie Sleigh in the Mersey 1864 – Henry Melling. (Courtesy Williamson Art Gallery).

part of the Tranmere Infirmary, later Saint Catherine's Hospital. Although many of the original buildings have been demolished the hospital is still serving the community.

However in the 1860s hospitals were still erected by voluntary subscription. When, therefore, the Borough Hospital was opened Birkenhead was fortunate to have a generous donor in John Laird, and in 1869 it was through the efforts of Doctor Braidwood that a much needed Children's Hospital was started in Wilkinson Street. After a number of moves it finally occupied the building, begun in 1882, in Woodchurch Road, which, although it is still standing, is no longer used for its original purpose.

In 1870 John Laird, the town's great benefactor, again showed his generosity by presenting a School of Art, building it adjacent to the Hospital near the Park Entrance. His death in 1874 ended the career of an outstanding personality whose loss was mourned throughout the Borough. Shortly afterwards, in 1876, Sir William Jackson, another outstanding personality, also died. He had been a tireless worker for the welfare of the town and must have been remembered for his many achievements.

The greatest change of all, in the affairs of the town, came in 1877 with the granting of the Charter of Incorporation, when Birkenhead became a Borough with its own Town Council consisting of a Mayor, 14 Aldermen and 42 Councillors elected to represent nine wards. The first election took place on 14th November 1877 and returned 40 Conservatives and 2 Liberals. On 20th November the Town Council met for the first time in the Claughton Road Music Hall and John Laird Junior was elected the first Mayor.

A sidelight on the election day was that while the police were occupied with conducting the election, many of the townspeople took the opportunity to clean their chimneys by setting fire to them. It is recorded that the situation became so dangerous that many feared the whole town would be set alight.

Armorial Bearings and the Common Seal were granted to the new Borough in 1878. The Pastoral Staff and the Lion were part of the seal of the Extra Parochial Chapelry or Township of Birkenhead. The Oak Tree was chosen to represent Tranmere, the Star Bebington and the two Lions Oxton. The Crosier was part of the Prior's Arms. Canon Tarver of Chester suggested the motto which is "Ubi Fides ibi Lux et Robur" . . . Where there is faith there is light and strength.

The Mayoral Regalia was acquired over a period of years. In 1878 McGregor Laird presented the Mayor's Badge and Chain in gold, with the Borough Arms and Crest in enamel on the Badge and Sir

Elliott Lees donated the Mace, in silver gilt, in 1897 in commemoration of the Diamond Jubilee of Queen Victoria. The Mayoress's Badge and Chain in gold set with emeralds and diamonds were presented by ex-mayoresses of Birkenhead to mark the coronation of Edward VII in 1902 and the Deputy Mayor's Badge was given by William H. Egan in 1940, during his first term of office as Mayor.

Since the Mayor of Wirral uses the Wallasey Regalia, some of the Birkenhead collection can now be seen on display in the Williamson Art Gallery.

The town continued to develop, but the early rapid pace had changed to one of slower, steady progress. The Abattoirs and Tannery had been established over thirty years when, in 1878, the Gelatine and Glue Works were built near the entrance to Tranmere Pool by Thompson Brothers. At first they made use of the available waste material from the Tannery, but as the business expanded the local supply had to be supplemented from other sources. Over the years new processes have been introduced, but although these long established works have been enlarged, to allow for this, they still stand on their original site.

Within the next two years further progress was made in transport. Monks Ferry was closed and Woodside Station was opened in 1878 connecting the ferry with the railway and providing a main line service to London. The station building was regarded as a fine example of Victorian Railway Architecture, but was demolished in 1967. In 1879, the year following the opening of the station, the luggage boat service was begun with a floating roadway and landing stage. The first luggage boat was the Oxton and the service continued for many years.

By 1879 thousands of cattle were being imported through Birkenhead from the U.S.A. To prevent any disease being carried to herds in this country it was necessary to examine these animals on arrival and so the Lairages, which were large sheds containing cattle pens, were erected to provide them with shelter during this period of examination. The site chosen was next to Woodside Ferry. In the 1820s Sir Richard Puleston's pretty villa had stood there. Henry Aspinal tells us that Sir Richard was fond of summer cruising on the river and round the Welsh coast. "During the summer his yacht was anchored opposite his house, near the existing pontoon bridge for goods traffic." This was apparently a safe anchorage with deep water and therefore suitable in later years for cargo ships.

John Laird Jn., Birkenhead's first Mayor, 1877. (Courtesy Wiliamson Art Gallery).

The early Commissioners had, with great foresight, provided the Park and in 1881 the Town Council, pursuing a similar policy, acquired forty-five acres of Thurstaston Common as an open space for ". . . the purpose of exercise and recreation for the benefit of the inhabitants of Thurstaston, Birkenhead and neighbourhood." They also purchased twenty-one acres on Tranmere Hill which was laid out as parkland and opened to the public in 1885 as Mersey Park.

1882 saw the opening of the Argyle Street South Baths. They provided a swimming bath plus slipper, shower and vapour baths and proved to be very popular, the swimming bath being reserved at certain times for ladies only.

On 26th July 1882 Birkenhead was granted a Court of Quarter Sessions and in 1884 the Sessions Court was built at the rear of the new Town Hall, being opened in 1887 by William Laird. A further step in the town's development occurred in 1888 when, through the Local Government Act, it became a County Borough.

After a delay of nearly fifty years the foundation stone of the new Town Hall had been laid in 1883 by the Mayor, Alderman T.S. Deakin. It was an imposing building in Storeton stone, Scottish granite and marble and was erected on the site which had been reserved for it in Hamilton Square. Four years later on 10th February 1887 John Laird, who had been the first Mayor, performed the opening ceremony before an assembly of some five thousand people. The building with its clock tower nearly 200 feet high was designed by C.O. Ellison and Son of Liverpool and was chosen from 138 entries submitted in open competition. Some years ago the exterior was cleaned and the stone restored to its original pleasing colour, and Birkonians saw their Town Hall as it had looked a century ago.

The year 1986 saw the centenary of the opening of the Mersey Railway on 21st January 1886 by H.R.H. the Prince of Wales. The original line was from Green Lane, through Central and Hamilton Square stations to James Street, Liverpool. Since steam trains were used the atmosphere was smoky and unpleasant, but the journey was quick and not influenced by weather conditions. The fare from Hamilton Square to James Street was one penny and the journey became more pleasant in 1903 when the railway was electrified. The number of passengers on the ferry boats was reduced, but the ferries remained popular and profitable. The new trains proved to be very popular and some time later the lines were extended to Rock Ferry and West Kirby.

As we have seen, in the early days of the town, Chester Street was not only a main highway to Chester and Wirral it was also a busy shopping centre. The Market was close by in Hamilton Street and Argyle Street was described as, ". . . the premier thoroughfare, and the shopping centre of the principal residents of the district", but the extension of the railway to Woodside had an adverse affect on trade and changed the prosperity of the locality. In his memoirs J.R. Kaighin tells us, "With baskets heavy laden, country folk made their way down Ivy Street to the railway station. Its removal to Woodside altered and dislocated the trading conditions of Chester Street, (it became so convenient to take the ferry boats to Liverpool), which were subsequently further worsened by the network of tramlines established and the opening of the Mersey Railway. Chester Street seriously declined as a trading centre."

For a number of years residents had been moving away from the southern end of town, with Claughton, Oxton and Tranmere continuing to be favourite residential areas, and as Chester Street declined as a shopping centre so Grange Lane, because it was more central, grew in popularity. It was in 1860 that John Allanson and his sister opened their draper's shop there, opposite Saint Werburgh's Church. The shop prospered and remaining on the same site became a large store. In 1872 two brothers, George and Thomas Robb opened their draper's shop at 11 Cross Street. It also prospered and, following the trend shown by the population, moved in 1886 to a more promising site at the Charing Cross end of Grange Lane. The roadway had been widened about 1870 and the number of existing shops increased until Grange Lane became the acknowledged shopping centre for the town, with these two shops becoming two of the largest and most important. Allanson's is now Beatties, but Robb Brother's closed some years ago after more than a century of service.

Saint Mary's, as we have seen, was the first church to be built in Birkenhead and provided the first school, but as the population grew more churches, of all denominations, were built and most provided their own schools. There were also voluntary schools plus private establishments, but the major provision of education was denominational. In 1891 the population was 99,857 which included a large number of children of school age. The first Education Act had been passed in 1870 and from then onwards there had been pressure from certain residents advocating the formation of a School Board, but it was a pressure which had been successfully defeated in favour of sectarian education until 1893. In that year the Town Council decided in favour of appointing a School Board and in 1895 the first

Board School, the Woodlands, was built to be followed within a few years by Cathcart Street, Laird Street and Well Lane Schools.

The Public Library had proved to be very popular, but as the town expanded the distance between Hamilton Street and the outlying districts posed problems for borrowers, so in 1894 the first two branch libraries were opened. The North Branch was in Price Street and the South Branch in Grove Road, Rock Ferry.

The Police Force continued to combine fire fighting with their other duties until 1894 when a separate Fire Brigade was formed. We are told that in 1843 the police were issued with a Merryweather Fire Engine at a cost of £200 and horses were hired to pull it at five shillings per trip. The number of policemen increased over the years and in 1863 the first Chief Constable, Major Beswick, was appointed. With Incorporation in 1877 came re-organisation and the force of 136 constables was divided into four divisions; Town, Tranmere, Claughton and Docks, and in 1879 a fire station was opened in Tranmere and provided with an escape engine and ambulance. When fire fighting duties were finally relinquished the force was 147 and the number was not reduced. In 1899 as a further boost to their efficiency detectives were issued with bicycles.

The newly formed Fire Brigade had a professional Chief Fire Officer, Mr. W.J. Monk, formerly of the London Fire Brigade. In 1895 it moved into new headquarters, the purpose built Central Fire Station in Whetstone Lane which was provided with modern equipment.

The governing body in Birkenhead, from the first Commissioners onwards, had always been receptive to new ideas which would benefit the town. So when in 1895 the Corporation built an electricity generating station in Bentinck Street they were one of the first local authorities to do so and were following a tradition of "firsts" already established in Birkenhead's history. By the next year electricity was being supplied to a few consumers, but at first this new form of energy did not prove to be generally popular.

The introduction of electricity was a major undertaking which would influence the domestic and commercial scenes of the future, but the year 1895 was probably remembered by the inhabitants of the town for the severe weather conditions in January and February when the Mersey froze over. Contemporary photographs show that this was no exaggeration. The adverse weather conditions caused great difficulties when water pipes and even gas mains froze. Most outdoor work ceased, there were food shortages and the poorer people were suffering such distress that a relief fund was started, soup kitchens were provided and Alderman Gamlin, with the help of the police, organised the distribution of thousands of loaves of bread. There was, nevertheless, a lighter side to the winter because during the frost the Park remained open day and night to enable skaters to use the frozen lakes. Oil lamps and candles illuminated the scene with braziers on the lake sides providing a little warmth.

Following the policy of providing open spaces the Corporation decided to acquire Bidston Hill and the first acres of land were purchased from Mr. Robert Vyner in 1894. The plan was continued and developed until eventually some 140 acres had been bought. The 20 acres of pine woods were designated a memorial to Mr. Edmund Taylor in recognition of his work for the scheme. Because of the foresight of these early councillors the hill with its unspoiled beauty still provides a natural habitat for wildlife and provides the walker with panoramic views across the estuaries of the Mersey and the Dee.

The horse-drawn trams had served the town for nearly forty years when in 1897 a group of town councillors visited Blackpool, Bristol and the French town of Rouen to observe their electric tramway systems. When they returned their enthusiasm was such that another generating station was built in Craven Street and by February 1901 the first electric tram ran from Woodside to New Ferry. Within two years all the horse-drawn trams had been replaced with the newer, bigger, quicker and, after dark, brightly lit electric trams.

The ferries had always been important to Birkenhead and so when about 1897 the Rock Ferry Company ran into difficulties and the ferries ceased to operate they were taken over by the Birkenhead Corporation who had acquired the South End or New Ferry to Liverpool service about the same time. The New Ferry service was re-commenced by Birkenhead in 1897 and, having constructed a pier with a floating landing stage at Rock Ferry, the service from there was re-commenced in 1899.

By the end of the 19th century Liverpool, including Birkenhead, had, under the management of the Mersey Docks and Harbour Board, become a prosperous port of major importance. The dock systems had been extended on both sides of the river and in 1891 when John Masefield joined the Conway he saw, "... a river full of ships of all sorts; two cities full of ships of all sorts ... In the docks on both sides were masts, sails, flags of ships in fifties and hundreds."

The years between 1840-60 had seen many changes both commercial and financial. During those years emigration to America, via Liverpool to New York, reached its peak. Some of the emigrants came from the continent, but most were from the British

The Town Hall, opened 1887.

Isles. Then after the discovery of gold in Australia in 1852, a fresh wave of emigration reached such proportions that the Government opened depots and chartered special sailing ships to cope with the situation. There was a depot in Liverpool and another in Birkenhead.

The first lighthouse was built on Bidston Hill about 1771 and a few years earlier the Signal Station had been established. This consisted of a number of flagstaffs on which were displayed the house flags of vessels as they approached the Mersey. The Government had established a number of these stations between Bidston and Holyhead and messages could be received in Liverpool, in the grounds of Saint Nicholas' Church, within eight minutes thus alerting the shipowners to the imminent arrival of their vessels. In 1847 an electric telegraph was installed in Liverpool and the Signal Station was no longer required, but the lighthouse continued to operate until 1872 when it was replaced by the present structure which operated until 1913.

In 1830 the unsatisfactory Rock Perch Beacon which was made of wood and stood on Perch Rock, was also replaced by the present lighthouse at New Brighton also on Perch Rock. The Fort was part of the original plan, but was built at a later date.

The Observatory was first established in Liverpool for meteorological studies, but was transferred in 1867 to Bidston Hill. From then onwards it also operated the One O'clock Gun which was fired daily as a time check for mariners, giving Greenwich mean time. The original gun was from the Crimean War, the second, a smaller version, came from Woolwich Arsenal, but this was eventually replaced by a small six pounder. The gun was sited on the river front at Morpeth Pier and when it was fired people on the Liverpool waterfront saw the puff of smoke almost four seconds before they heard the report. The custom of firing it was discontinued in 1969 and the loss of its familiar boom was regretted by many of the residents of Birkenhead. The Observatory now houses the Institute of Coastal Oceanography and Tides and is the world's principal source of tidal information.

The Bidston Windmill must also have been a landmark for sailors. The existence of a wooden peg mill was recorded in 1609, but this was destroyed by fire in 1791 and was replaced by the present brick structure in 1821. It ceased to operate in 1875, but fortunately was restored in 1894, as a monument, by Mr. R.S. Hudson. It is an interesting reminder of the past in a town which became an important milling centre.

Liverpool's trade with the East had increased with the abolition of the East India Company's monopolies, first with India in 1813 and later with China in 1833 and the opening of the Suez Canal in 1869, giving a shorter route to the East, further increased that trade. Improved communications also played their part in the financial success of the port, the electric telegraph in 1847 being followed in 1866 by the laying of the great Atlantic cable joining England to America.

Henry Aspinall in his memoirs contrasted the river of his childhood, clear and sparkling with sandy beaches, with the Mersey's appearance later in the century, "The building of sea walls and docks on each side has narrowed the stream and brought into being a rapid current." He also described the surface of the water as no longer smooth and clear, but broken and thick and told how the beautiful seaweed which once covered the beach from New Brighton to Eastham had given way to dirty grass and mud.

By the end of the century all traces of the headland had disappeared. There was no longer a Tranmere Pool and Wallasey Pool had become the Birkenhead Docks, while the river frontage was dominated by ship building and its associated industries.

Steam was replacing sail in ships and the big shipping lines were emerging. Many of these lines sailed so regularly from Birkenhead that they had berths reserved for them. Some of the well known names associated with Birkenhead were, the Blue Funnel, Bibby, Anchor, Ellerman and Hall, Brocklebank, Clan City, Henderson and Harrison Lines and most of them traded with India or the far East.

With ships coming into the port from many countries precautions had to be taken against the introduction of infectious diseases and so the Lazarettos were introduced into the Mersey. They were quarantine ships, old wooden sailing vessels, spacious and very comfortable and were moored off Rock Ferry. Ships entering the Mersey had to report any sickness on board, or in any of their ports of call, by hoisting a yellow flag. The ship then proceeded to anchor as near as possible to the Lazarettos and was not allowed to dock until the Medical Officer of Health had visited it and declared it free from infection.

Shipping lines needed officers and crew and by the end of the 19th century four sailing frigates had come to the river as training ships for the Merchant Navy. They were the Conway, Akbar, Indefatigable and the Clarence, and were also moored in the Sloyne off Rock Ferry. The two most famous were the Conway, for training boys as officers, and the Indefatigable where boys were trained for the lower decks. Stella M. Pinches tells us, "Speech days and prize givings on Conway and Indefatigable were great occasions as were also the visits of the Channel Fleet when firework displays were held on the river."

Three ships held the name Conway and the last was originally H.M.S. Nile launched in 1839 and brought to the Mersey in 1876. In 1941, during the Second World War, she was taken to the Menai Straits and it was in 1953 when she was being towed to Liverpool for a refit that she ran aground and broke her back.

6

The 20th Century

At the beginning of the 19th century the population of Birkenhead was 110 persons. A hundred years later in 1901 it numbered 110,915. Almost all traces of the original hamlet had disappeared and the street plan, with houses and shops plus many of the public buildings familiar to-day, was already established and shipbuilding and the docks, with other related industries, still occupied the majority of the workforce.

The Corporation continued to consider plans for improvement and development and in October 1900 the Livingstone Street Baths were opened, the first class swimming bath being reserved for ladies each evening, except Wednesdays and Saturdays, when mixed bathing was allowed.

In 1901, the year in which Queen Victoria died, pursuing the policy of providing open spaces for recreation, a further 29 acres were acquired on Tranmere Hill and became Victoria Park where one of the attractions is the 15th century Tranmere Cross. It originally stood in the village street, but about 1862 disappeared. It was subsequently found in the grounds of Tranmere New Hall, presented to the Corporation and in 1937 re-erected in the new park at the Church Road entrance.

Unfortunately the new Town Hall was severely damaged by fire in 1901 causing the clock tower to collapse. Other parts of the building were also damaged and the repair bill amounted to £15,000. When the tower was restored the design was altered and the damaged window on the staircase was replaced by one which depicted Edward 1st's visit to the Priory in 1277.

Education had been directed by the School Board for ten years when, in accordance with the Education Act of 1902, it was replaced in 1903 by an Education Committee. The provisions of the Act stated that the Local Authority was responsible for providing adequate elementary education and so a number of schools were built prior to 1914 and the First World War. Some of the schools included in that programme were; Mersey Park, Woodchurch Road, Hemingford Street, Brassey Street, Rock Ferry, Temple Road and Bidston Avenue and during the war Bidston Avenue and Hemingford Street

The Eleanor Cross erected in memory of Queen Victoria, 1905.

were used as temporary hospitals for the wounded. With some modifications, to conform to modern standards, all these schools are still in use to-day with the exception of Brassey Street and Hemingford Street where the buildings are now used for other purposes.

Another war which had involved Birkenhead men was the Second Boer War which lasted for four years and ended in 1902. The names of those who served as volunteers with the Cheshire Regiment during the conflict are recorded on brass tablets on the posts at the foot of the staircase in the Town Hall.

The establishing of industry so near to Hamilton Square lessened its desirability as a residential area and in 1903 the Corporation acquired the central private garden and opened it to the public. It was laid out in the manner familiar to us to-day. John Laird's statue faced the Town Hall and the Eleanor Cross in the centre was erected two years later as a memorial to Queen Victoria. Queen Eleanor was the wife of Edward 1st and when she died similar crosses were erected to mark the places where her funeral procession had stopped overnight. The graceful monument in the Square was designed by Edmund Kirby of Birkenhead and remembering Edward 1st's connection with the Priory, would appear to have been a very pertinent choice. To-day John Laird's statue stands on the west side of the Square and facing the Town Hall is the Cenotaph erected in 1925 to the memory of those men who lost their lives in the First World War, 1914-18.

The library service had become so popular that ten years after the opening of the two branch libraries more space and better facilities were needed and the Corporation decided to approach Andrew Carnegie. His help was forthcoming and he built a new Central Library, next to the Market, and rebuilt the two branches. When they were opened in 1909 the Central Library building won general admiration for its great architectural merit and was one of the finest buildings in the town.

The General Post Office, also needing more adequate premises, moved from Conway Street in 1907 to the present building in Argyle Street. The old building became the Super Cinema and is now used as a warehouse. It has always been remembered as the scene of an unsolved crime when the caretaker, George Fell, was murdered there on 9th September 1900.

General Baden-Powell came to Birkenhead in 1908 to deliver a lecture, in the YMCA Hall in Grange Road, on his experiences during the South African War. It was during that meeting that the Boy Scout Movement was inaugurated and a commemorative

The General Post Office, opened 1907.

plaque, unveiled by the Chief Scout in 1910, commemorates the event. The plaque is now displayed in the YMCA building in Whetstone Lane and reads:— "In this hall the Boy Scout Movement was publicly inaugurated by Lieut. General Sir Robert S.S. Baden-Powell K.C.B. on January 24th 1908."

In 1929, to celebrate the 21st anniversary of the movement, a World Jamboree, attended by the Prince of Wales, was held in Arrowe Park which had been acquired by the Corporation in 1927. 50,000 scouts from countries of many nations came together in companionship for two weeks. A life size sculpture of a scout, by E. Carter Preston of Liverpool, stands in Arrowe Park as a reminder of this great occasion.

Birkenhead again showed a forward looking policy when in 1909 a petrol driven fire engine, one of the first in the country, was supplied to the Fire Brigade, which shortly afterwards became fully mechanised.

When the Lairages were first built they were necessary because thousands of cattle were being imported, but by the early years of the 20th century the cattle trade had dwindled, because frozen meat was easier to handle. Therefore many animals were being slaughtered in their country of origin. In 1912 an outbreak of Foot and Mouth Disease in Ireland changed the situation. Irish cattle, which previously had been imported through many ports throughout the country, were directed to one port of entry only and Birkenhead was chosen for this purpose. The Lairages at Morpeth and Wallasey Docks, officially known as the Mersey Cattle Wharf, were busy again for many years, but have now fallen into disuse.

Edward VII's short reign ended in 1910. The Clock Tower, or King's Clock as it is commonly called, was erected to his memory and was unveiled in 1912. It originally stood nearer the Central Station in Wilbraham Street, in front of the former Saint Paul's School, but was later moved to its present position in Clifton Crescent.

1919 saw a significant addition to passenger transport within the town when, on 12th July, the first motor bus service ran from Rock Ferry to Park Station. Soon ten buses were operating and as the trams declined in popularity so buses took over on all routes. On 17th July 1937 the last tram made its final journey on the Oxton Claughton Circular Route. Birkenhead had always kept in pace with modern development in transport and adopted covered double-deck buses ahead of other towns. In 1970 the Merseyside Passenger Transport Authority took control of the buses and the ferries, but on 26th October 1986 deregulation of the buses took place and the

The Clock Tower, erected in memory of King Edward VII, 1912. Central Station in the background.

services were divided among a number of companies.

Woodside Ferry is the only surviving service of the many ferries which once plied across the river from Birkenhead. The electrified Mersey Railway and electric trams, followed by the buses, all drew passengers away from the New Ferry and Rock Ferry services which were finally closed as unprofitable. The New Ferry boats in 1932 and the ones from Rock Ferry on 30th June 1939.

The Mersey Railway and the tunnel now offer speedy means of transport to the centre of Liverpool, but although there have, at times, been proposals to close Woodside, the ancient ferry has always survived. Over the years the most up to date types of ferry boats have been used. In 1960 the steam ferry boats were replaced by a new diesel fleet, Mountwood, Woodchurch and Overchurch and recently the landing stage was completely overhauled. It is many years now since the Liverpool Charter was sold to a private company and later bought by the Birkenhead Corporation giving Birkenhead the right of ferriage in both directions. This explains why fares for both journeys are paid in Birkenhead.

The luggage boats had provided the only means of communication between Birkenhead and Liverpool for horse-drawn and motor traffic, but as the amount of motor traffic increased long queues formed and better communication was obviously needed.

There were two possibilities, a tunnel or a bridge, and eventually after much discussion the joint Corporations of Liverpool and Birkenhead decided in favour of a tunnel. Work began on this major undertaking in 1925 with construction crews working from both ends. In 1928 the two tunnels met and the Lord Mayor of Liverpool and the Mayor of Birkenhead greeted each other, but the luggage boats were not taken out of service until 1941, although they stopped taking motor vehicles when the road tunnel was opened. The all night ferry boat service was cancelled in 1956 and replaced by buses through the tunnel.

In Birkenhead a number of buildings had to be demolished to make way for the tunnel entrance and one of these was regretably the Central Library built by Andrew Carnegie. The stock was moved back into the former library in Hamilton Street pending the erection of a new building.

By 1934 the tunnel was finished and an impressive new library stood in Borough Road. On 18th July King George V and Queen Mary officially opened the tunnel by driving through and in Queen Mary's honour, the new underground roadway was named

'Queensway'. The Royal Couple then proceeded to the new Central Library where the King performed the opening ceremony.

The library service continued to be popular and as the town expanded, new branches were built to cater for the needs of the community in the outlying districts.

Work on the tunnel did not end with the official opening. The number of vehicles using it increased rapidly and to overcome traffic congestion within the town, the Approaches Scheme was devised in 1964 by the Borough Engineer, Mr. H.C. Oxburgh. When this was completed and opened, in 1969, tunnel traffic was separated from town traffic and the entry and exit facilities improved.

In 1927 Birkenhead celebrated its Jubilee as a Borough, 1877-1927, and it was fitting that this anniversary should occur at a time of achievement and expansion. Arrowe Park was acquired in that year. Work on the new tunnel was well advanced and within a few years a new Central Library would be built, with 1928 seeing the completion of the Williamson Art Gallery and Museum. This stands at the junction of Slatey Road and Balls Road and the architects were Leonard and Herbert Theale. The Gallery was erected through the generosity of John Williamson, a director of the Cunard Shipping Company, and his son Patrick who, between them, bequeathed £40,000 to the Corporation of Birkenhead for a project of this type. It houses many fine collections including an outstanding one of English Water Colours. Other collections include some fine examples of Wedgewood, Worcester and Minton china. The Della Robia ceramics were manufactured in Birkenhead and Liverpool Pottery is featured in the Knowles Boney Collection. Of particular interest to students of local history are the exhibits in the Maritime and Birkenhead Galleries.

The Birkenhead Docks, begun in 1844, took nearly ninety years to complete. In 1928 the river entrance was widened and deepened thus giving better facilities for the larger vessels engaged in trade with the East. In the same year Lord Derby formally opened the entrance lock to the Alfred Dock and by 1933 with the finishing of the Bidston Dock the Birkenhead Dock Estate, comprising nine miles of docking facilities, reached completion.

A further centre for indoor recreation was also completed in 1933 when Byrne Avenue Baths, Rock Ferry, were opened.

In the late 1930s the international situation was troubled and by 1939 war was imminent. Therefore, on Saturday 2nd September, thousands of school children accompanied by their teachers,

Conway Street 1914. (Courtesy Williamson Art Gallery). The Conway Arms on the left was at the junction with Claughton Road.

gathered in Woodside Station and were taken by train to undisclosed destinations, mostly in North Wales and Shropshire. All carried their gas masks, in small cardboard boxes, slung across one shoulder. The Committees in the reception areas were ready to receive them and so the evacuation took place and Birkenhead became a town virtually without children. The next morning, Sunday 3rd September, war was declared.

The Merchant and Naval vessels of the Atlantic convoys used the Birkenhead and Liverpool Docks, so Merseyside was an important target area for enemy bombers. Residents of Birkenhead became accustomed to the wail of the sirens and learned to dread clear moonlit nights. There were no air raids during the first few months, but it was the lull before the storm and when the enemy action came it caused many deaths and severe damage. Between August 1940 and November 1941, 464 people were killed. Some 2079 houses were destroyed and more than 26,000 badly damaged, but the "March Blitz", the night of 12th-13th March 1941, was the raid most readily remembered when, during eight hours, 40 land mines and 180 heavy bombs were dropped causing 288 deaths. During those war years the people of the town were not lacking in bravery, resilience and comradeship and when the war ended in 1945, Birkenhead officially celebrated by illuminating Hamilton Square Gardens and the Town Hall. After years of blackout it was a wonderful sight which brought visitors from many outlying districts to join in our celebrations.

After moving to the river front, Laird's shipyard continued to prosper, always maintaining a forward looking policy. Between 1870 and 1900 a total of 270 ships were built and 1903 saw a merger with the firm of Charles Cammell and Company, the Sheffield steel firm from which Laird's obtained its steel plating. This resulted in a major extension to the yard and in 1920 the M.V. Fullager was built, the first ever all welded ship and thus the Birkenhead firm scored another notable first in the history of ship building.

From the beginning of the 20th century Laird's had established a reputation for building naval vessels and in 1935 work began on H.M.S. Ark Royal, the first ship built as an aircraft carrier. 1938 saw the launch of the Cunard luxury liner Mauretania, 33,000 tons, and this was followed in 1939 by the battleship Prince of Wales, 35,000 tons. The Trident class submarine Thetis was also launched in 1939, but sank in Liverpool Bay during her sea trials with a considerable loss of life and only four survivors.

Laird's contribution to the war effort was outstanding. During those six years they built 106 naval vessels and carried out repairs on 9 battleships, 11 aircraft carriers and 2,000 merchant ships.

Throughout its history, Laird's has experienced both prosperity and recession and the firm's title has been re-styled a number of times, but it has always survived the periods of recession. The post war years brought prosperity and major modernisation schemes. Two of the most famous vessels of the 1960s were the Polaris submarines H.M.S. Renown and H.M.S. Revenge. The yard now has some of the most advanced technical facilities available plus a covered construction hall where ships can be built and fitted.

The present world recession in shipping has brought difficulties. The yard is now amalgamated with Vickers of Barrow-in-Furness, but with a much reduced work force, plus recent orders for a Royal Naval frigate and submarines for which it is justly famous. Its survival is assured for the immediate future, and the workforce has recently been increased.

When the war was over, Birkenhead could once again look forward and a priority task was to remove the scars of war. Air raid shelters disappeared. Temporary pre-fabricated homes were erected. Houses were rebuilt and bombed sites cleared of rubble. Albeit with a number of empty spaces the town presented a reasonably normal appearance again.

When peace finally came, however, two familiar pre-war features were absent from the streets. Before the war the Haymarket was a popular Saturday evening meeting place where self appointed orators, standing on improvised platforms, vigorously expressed their views on all subjects, Birkenhead's own equivalent of Hyde Park Corner. It was a noisy diversion because the Salvation Army also held a weekly meeting there, with hymns and band vieing with the speakers.

The Liverpool fruit sellers, wending their way through the streets of houses, were a picturesque sight, reminders of earlier times and customs. They wore a distinctive style of dress with many petticoats and a large woven shawl in grey or black and were known locally as "Mary Ellens". The fruit, usually oranges and lemons, was carried on their heads in big shallow baskets and their cry of, "Oranges and lemons", was a familiar one still remembered by older residents.

A major project delayed by the war was quickly re-considered. From 1938 the supply of electricity had come from the Grid system, but immediately prior to the war proposals had reached an advanced stage to build a new generating station at Bromborough and the foundation stone of this new station was finally laid in 1948. The work was completed in 1953, but because of the nationalisation of the electricity industry it became part of the Merseyside and North

Wales Electricity Board.

In 1950 the foundation stone of the Technical College, in Borough Road, was laid by Queen Elizabeth, now the Queen Mother. This was the fulfilment of a plan first suggested in 1866, but for various reasons postponed many times. The building was completed in 1955 and opened by Lord Cohen of Birkenhead. Since then additional buildings and facilities have been added and the official handbook of 1974 states, "Today the College of Technology can offer full-time day and part-time day and evening courses in a wide range of technical and commercial-subjects and special emphasis is given to courses most closely related to the main industries and occupations in the area."

From the beginning of this century the Town Council had supported plans for better housing conditions and new homes were built in different areas, but it was in the post war years that the movement to reduce overcrowding by slum clearance gathered momentum and 1949 saw the official opening of the extensive Woodchurch Estate, which in 1950 gained a Ministry of Health Diploma. There has also been re-development within the town and there are now two more new estates at Ford and Noctorum.

As the population has moved to the new estates on the perimeter of the town, so new schools have been provided to serve these areas. Of the many pioneer Church of England Schools in use during the last century, only four remain; Saint Saviour's, Christchurch and those in the ancient parishes of Bidston and Woodchurch. Within the town and on the new estates the Roman Catholic churches still retain their parochial schools, but in every case all these denominational schools are now housed in modern, pleasant buildings. Throughout the town schools have been adapted to meet current requirements of re-organisation and have followed contemporary educational philosophy and practice.

Some of the long established schools still remain:— Holt Hill Convent moved from smaller premises in 1856 to the house on Holt Hill, formerly owned by the Reverend William Sewell, vicar of Saint Oswald's, Bidston. A house with extensive grounds. It amalgamated in 1976 with Heathley High School to become the new Marian High School which now occupies the premises of the former Noctorum High School. The convent buildings have been demolished and the site used for housing development. The school has recently been renamed Saint Benedicts.

Birkenhead School, with its record of illustrious former pupils, began in 1860 in Royden House, Park Road North, but by 1870 had moved to its present site in Shrewsbury Road, where in the course of time new buildings have been erected.

The Tranmere High School opened in 1882, but closed in 1939 through financial difficulties.

Birkenhead Insitute was opened in 1889 in Whetstone Lane and is now housed in the former Grange Secondary School in Tollemache Road.

Birkenhead High School for Girls still occupies the house Belgrano in Devonshire Road where it began in 1901. To meet the needs of the growing number of pupils new buildings have been erected and the school is run by The Girls' Public Day School Trust.

The Birkenhead Secondary School for Girls opened in Conway Street in 1906, but moved to Park Road South in 1929 where a new school had been built on the former site of a large house, Beechfield. At that time the the name was changed to Park High School for Girls. In recent years it has combined with Park High School for Boys, in Park Road North, as a comprehensive school.

Saint Anselm's College is the newest school catering for boys up to sixth form level and was founded in the 1930s in a large house in Egerton Road, formerly owned by a Mr. William Heap. To cater for its 700 pupils extensive new buildings have been added to the original house.

A notable event for the year 1953 was the opening, by Sir David Maxwell Fyfe, of the new Police Headquarters at the junction of Mortimer Street and Chester Street, the building being extended in 1956 by another wing. From the 1830s the history of the Force was one of expansion and development. Despite the difficulties of the war years, modernisation was undertaken from 1943 onwards. Women constables had a special role to fulfil and the introduction of cars with wireless communication was in great contrast to the first issue of bicycles in 1898. Another modern development was the introduction of a dog section with six Alsations. Traffic Wardens were first appointed in 1965 and in the same year personal radios were issued to officers, but in 1967 the Birkenhead Borough Police Force was amalgamated with the Forces of Wallasey, Stockport, Chester and Cheshire County to become the Cheshire County Constabulary. From 1986, after the abolition of the short lived Merseyside County Council, the Force became part of the Merseyside Police Authority.

Birkenhead has a long association with the oil industry and in 1960 this was further developed when the Tranmere Crude Oil Terminal was opened. It was a combined venture between the Mersey Docks

The Williamson Art Gallery and Museum. (Courtesy Williamson Art Gallery and Museum).

and Harbour Company and the Shell Refining Company and they chose a site adjacent to Cammell Laird's where, with a floating stage, large tankers can be handled. The Tank Farm is built on reclaimed land and the crude oil, many thousands of tons per day, is transported to the Stanlow Oil Refinery, the whole project requiring a considerable workforce.

By 1970 there were few people left living in the vicinity of Saint Mary's and the congregation was therefore considerably reduced so the church was closed, but when it was demolished the tower was left standing. The peal of six bells could always be heard clearly across the town and the river. They were rung in 1844 to celebrate the laying of the foundation stone for the Docks and were subsequently rung on all important occasions until 1970. When they were removed in 1976 the Birkenhead History Society purchased one bell and presented it to the Williamson Art Gallery where it is known as the Knox Bell. The inscription on the bell reads:—

"Glory be to God on High
Peace on earth and
Goodwill towards men.
Alleluyah"

A number of names are also inscribed:—

John Taylor, Oxford, Campanarius.
George Gillibrand, Liverpool, Church
Bell Hanger.
The Right Reverend John Sumner D.D.
Lord Bishop of Chester.
Francis Richard Price Esq.
Lord of the Manor and Patron.
The Reverend Andrew Knox, Minister.

The meaning of the decoration round the rim is not clear.

Building a new Fire Brigade and Ambulance Service Headquarters was to be one of the Birkenhead Council's last major works before becoming part of the Wirral community. On 28th March 1973 the new headquarters at the junction of Exmouth Street and Claughton Road were officially opened and the town acquired a modern building designed for functional and administrative efficiency.

Birkenhead had received its Charter of Incorporation in 1877, but nearly a hundred years later in April 1974 it ceased to be an independent Local Authority when it became part of the Metropolitan Borough of Wirral. It therefore also became part of the much larger Merseyside County Council, but this had a short life and was abolished on 1st April 1986. For the newly formed Council in Wirral, Wallasey Town Hall became the administrative centre.

As part of the community of Wirral, the town elects its own councillors for local administration, but shares the benefits provided on a wider scale. Thus in 1978 H.M. Queen Elizabeth opened the modernised Mersey Railway, which was extended to provide a loop line with two new stations at Moorfields and Lime Street in Liverpool. Four years later in 1982 the Arrowe Park Hospital was opened, providing modern medical facilities within a large building in a semi-rural area.

It is a short 170 years since 1821 when the first commuter settled in Birkenhead, in the house he had built on the river front. In that short time the town has grown rapidly. There have been periods of recession and periods of great progress, but recent years have seen a serious decline in shipping and the once busy docks, although still used, are busy no longer, but long established firms in the dock area and on the river front still form part of the industrial pattern. Shipbuilding, ship repairs, towing, precision engineering and other industries related to shipping, plus tanning, milling, the production of animal foodstuffs, oil and sugar, all provide employment, while newer industries related to modern technology and consumer requirements have been established.

With the changing pattern of industry the land on either side of Woodside Ferry is being redeveloped, thus giving residents access to the river front. The refurbished Ferry Terminal is now an information centre and cafe while the adjacent site of the former lairages is occupied by Woodside Business Park. A new bus station has transformed the approach to the Ferry Terminal and it is planned that the pleasant Riverside Walk will eventually extend from Monks Ferry to Seacombe. Other proposals include garden, residential and leisure areas plus a scheme to clear the river of pollution. Perhaps by the 21st century marine life will return to the Mersey and birch trees will grow again on Birchen Head.

The Headland 1991. (Courtesy John Mills Photography) and Merseyside Development Corporation reclaimed land north of Woodside obscures the mouth of Wallasey Pool. South of the Ferry the shipyard installations plus the reclaimed land for the Oil Terminal completely alter the natural contour of the river bank. Tranmere Pool has disappeared.

7

Personalities

In the early days of the rapidly expanding township of Birkenhead a number of its new residents played prominent parts in its development both commercially and politically. In this context the Laird family held a unique position over three generations. William Laird was born in Greenock in 1780. He married about 1804 and his wife, Agnes McGregor, was a direct descendant of Ronald, second son of Rob Roy. In 1810 he came to Liverpool to seek orders for his father's rope works in Greenock. He was not successful in this respect, but using his talents in other ways became a director of several steam packet companies. He also started an agency for James Watt's steam engine and bought a sugar house. Certainly a man of diverse interests. In 1824 he moved to Birkenhead and opened the boiler, and later shipbuilding yard, by Wallasey Pool which was to become the town's biggest industry. He lived in Cathcart Street near the yard, but was a town planner as well as a shipbuilder and it was he who, having bought a large area of land in the centre of the town, commissioned Gillespie Graham to draw up plans for its development. He later moved to number 63 in the elegant Hamilton Square where he died in 1841.

William's eldest son John was born in Greenock in 1805 so came to Liverpool as a small child and was educated at Liverpool Royal Institution. He was a solicitor and a member of the Institution of Naval Architects becoming his father's partner in 1828.

In spite of great prejudice, father and son were pioneers in the building of iron ships and after his father's death John Laird continued a forward looking policy. He moved the yard to Tranmere Pool in 1856 and two years later built his first steel ship, the Ma Robert.

He had always been keenly interested in the affairs of the town and was one of the first Commissioners in 1833 and when Birkenhead was made a Parliamentary Borough in 1861 he retired from the yard and became its first Member of Parliament. His sons John and William were already assisting him in the administration of the yard and after his retirement they were joined by their brother Henry.

No one played a more prominent and praiseworthy role in the

affairs of the town which was much indebted to him as a generous benefactor. Saint James' Church was founded and endowed by a number of prominent men which included John, McGregor and William Laird. He also personally provided the money to build the Borough Hospital and the Laird School of Art.

Hunting was a popular sport in the early days of the town and John Laird was a keen huntsman, but unfortunately a riding accident caused his death in 1874. In tribute to his memory the local paper was printed with black lines between the columns and many mourners followed his funeral procession to Saint Mary's where he was interred in the family tomb. As proof of the respect in which he was held his statue in Hamilton Square was erected by public subscription and unveiled by Lord Tollemache a fellow hunting enthusiast.

McGregor Laird was another of William's sons. He gained considerable fame as an African explorer and established the African Mail Company as well as being mainly responsible in founding the American Steam Navigation Company for the New York services, but he was also keenly interested and active in local affairs and as we have seen, was one of the founders of Saint James' Church. He lived in Hamilton Square where he was known for his friendly hospitality.

John and William Laird were two sons of John Laird senior who both took an active part in local politics and under their direction the shipyard maintained its fine traditions. When Birkenhead became a County Borough in 1877 John junior was the first Mayor, holding office for two consecutive years. His brother William followed him as Mayor also holding office for two consecutive years. Four years later John was Mayor again to be followed in the next year once more by brother William.

John died in 1898 and William in 1899 thus ending three generations of service to the town by members of this distinguished and respected family.

William Jackson was born in Warrington in 1805 the son of a well known doctor. He was the seventh son of his father Peter who was also a seventh son. When he was only five years old his father died and the family moved to Liverpool. In due course he was apprenticed to an ironmonger and having completed his training he opened his own shop. The business prospered and provided him with capital to engage in commerce and to become a partner in the firm of Hamilton, Jackson and Company and eventually he became closely associated with the African palm oil trade from which he accumulated a considerable fortune.

Unfortunately, while still in his thirties, his health gave cause for concern and so he retired from business in 1839, but after living in Italy for a period he recovered and took up residence in Birkenhead in Hamilton Square. He was a man of great vision and energy and like his brother John Somerville Jackson, whose monument in the form of an obelisk stands in Birkenhead Park, became deeply involved in the affairs of the emerging town, first as a Commissioner and later from 1842-46 as Chairman of the Commissioners.

In 1844 he purchased from Francis Price all his remaining property in Birkenhead which included Saint Mary's Church and the Manor of Claughton. Birket Hall, and the land surrounding it having been sold for development, William Jackson in 1846, built for himself a luxurious residence, Claughton Hall, in Egerton Road. In the early 1930's the Manor House and its extensive grounds were sold for urban development, the Manor Hill Estate.

He entered Parliament as a Liberal and served for nineteen years as member for Newcastle-under-Lyne. Later he represented North Derbyshire for several years. His business interests were not confined to Birkenhead. They were wide and varied including collieries and railway construction at home and abroad.

In 1866 at his own expense he erected the Albert Memorial Industrial Schools in Corporation Road as a memorial to the late Prince Consort and on the recommendation of the Prime Minister, W.E. Gladstone, in recognition of his political services, was knighted. In later life he left Birkenhead and died at his home in Portland Place, London, in 1876, but is buried in Flaybrick Hill Cemetery.

The families of Laird and Jackson were later united by marriage when Brigadier Geoffrey M. Jackson, grandson of Sir William, married John Laird's grand-daughter.

Thomas Brassey was born in 1805 at Bruera in the parish of Alford, Cheshire. He was a member of an ancient family of yeoman farmers with land at Bruera and Malpas. The young Thomas went to school in Chester and when he was sixteen he was articled to a Mr. Lawton, surveyor and land agent. He must have been a very able young man because at the early age of twenty one he became Mr. Lawton's partner and shortly afterwards was assigned to Birkenhead where the firm handled the affairs of Francis Richard Price, Lord of the Manor. Mr. Lawton died and he was appointed sole agent to Mr. Price. During the next few years the business prospered and soon he controlled brickworks, quarries and blacksmiths shops. He supplied the bricks for Liverpool's fifth Customs House, completed in 1839 and destroyed by enemy action during the Second World War. Also in the 1830s he constructed the New Chester Road from Tranmere to Bromborough.

When he met George Stephenson he was persuaded by him to tender for a section of railway then being constructed between Newton and Birmingham and the outcome was so successful that he was soon employed on other railways in the United Kingdom and other parts of the world. Sir Joseph Locke became his chief engineer and he built nearly all the French railways. He also built the Austrian railways and was decorated by the Emperor with the 'Iron Cross', but among his greatest achievements were the Caledonian Railway in Scotland and the railway between the Dardenelles and the Front Line during the Crimean War which he constructed at his own expense, to the great benefit of the fighting troops. He was also associated with the construction of the Grand Trunk Railway of Canada and for this project erected the Canada Works on the Great Float to build the rolling stock etc.. He is reputed to have, at one time, employed a work force of more than 40,000 men and is said to have been a remarkable personality, tolerant and compassionate with a flair for delegating responsibility to the right man and was respected by his employees for his trust and fair dealing.

During his early days in Birkenhead he met and married Maria, the second daughter of Joseph Harrison, who was the first commuter between Liverpool and Birkenhead. They lived at the corner of Grosvenor Road and Palm Grove where he built a house "Montana" which had pleasant gardens and some acres of land which he farmed, but because he was obliged to travel so extensively they eventually had many residences. Mrs. Brassey's sister Harriet Salt was the author of the delightful book of reminiscences "Birkenhead in its Infancy" and she lived at No. 73 Park Road South. Thomas and Maria had three sons all of whom had distinguished careers.

Two were Members of Parliament and the eldest was Chief Lord of the Admiralty and Governor of Victoria, Australia, later becoming Lord Brassey.

He died in 1870 at the age of sixty-five and is remembered by a memorial in Chester Cathedral which bears an inscription chosen by his sons. "Seeest thou a man diligent in business: he shall stand before kings."

Joseph Craven was born in Wakefield in 1820 and was a member of an old, respected Yorkshire family. Coming to Birkenhead in 1842 he established himself as an estate agent and as he prospered his business interests became wide and varied. The affairs of the emerging town soon claimed his interest and he took an active part in its development. It was through his financial expertise and foresight that the ferries which were running at a loss became profitable again.

He died in 1897 aged seventy-seven years having served the town in many ways. He was a magistrate and an active supporter of the Charter of Incorporation.

William Potter's name is frequently mentioned in the early history of Birkenhead. He lived in Oxton and was an important landowner, yet apart from references to him in public affairs there is little recorded information about him. He was keenly interested in the affairs of the town and proved himself a generous benefactor.

Together with William Jackson, John Laird and others, he was one of the group who conceived and initiated plans for the Docks in Birkenhead. He served as a Commissioner and in 1847 succeeded Sir William Jackson as Chairman.

At his own expence he provided two churches and schools; Saint Anne's Church and the Free Schools for 500 children adjoining it and Christchurch where the extensive crypts were designed as schools capable of taking 760 children. In partnership with a number of other prominent business men he was also responsible for building Saint James' Church and the schools attached to it.

The churches he erected still stand as reminders of his generosity and Christian spirit.

Henry Kelsall Aspinall published his memoirs, "Birkenhead and its Surroundings", in 1903 and in his book we find an eyewitness account of the growth of Birkenhead within his own lifetime from a small village to a large town.

John Aspinall, a ship owner, was one of the first residents to move from Liverpool after establishing the steam ferry boats. He came principally for the fox hunting and lived in a riverside villa, near Saint Mary's Church, where his son Henry was born in 1824. Since the total population in 1821 was only 200 and a survey in 1823 listed a mere 61 houses young Henry was born into a rural area, but by 1901 the population of the town had increased to 110,915 so he observed and was part of tremendous changes.

He gives an interesting account of life as he saw it during his boyhood days and later through mature eyes as an employer. He was a Brewer and became a Commissioner in 1854 and in the later role was instrumental in improving the ferry approaches. From him we receive personal and interesting glimpses of John Laird, Thomas Brassey and other notable figures of their day, well known to him.

When he died he was as old as the town which apparently appreciated his work in local politics since a street was named after him.

The Reverend Andrew Knox, Honorary Canon of Chester Cathedral, was born in 1797 and served in the army before entering the Church. He came to Saint Mary's as curate in 1828 and served as vicar from 1834-1881. When he arrived in 1828 the population of Birkenhead was 600 people, but when he attained his Jubilee at Saint Mary's in 1878 it had reached 85,000. He was a well known, respected and popular figure and, on the fortieth anniversary of his vicariate, he was presented with a purse of £1500 and medals were struck to commemorate the event.

In later years he was driven around the town in the pony carriage presented to him by his friends. It was often said that while John Laird made the town commercially Andrew Knox built it spiritually. He died in 1881 aged eighty four years and was buried, fittingly, in Saint Mary's.

Nearly a century later when Saint Mary's was demolished one of the bells was retained for posterity and in tribute to his memory was named "The Knox Bell".

Birkenhead Park was created through the skill and ingenuity of three men who transformed an unpromising area of land into a place of tranquil beauty.

Sir Joseph Paxton was born in 1801 the son of a Bedfordshire farmer, but he had a rare talent for gardening which was given scope when he went to work for the Duke of Devonshire at Chatsworth, serving there for thirty-two years and eventually becoming Head Gardener.

Although well known as a landscape gardener, he was also an architect designing many buildings and glass structures before completing his most famous work, the Crystal Palace, in 1854.

He had designed the Prince's Park development in Liverpool in 1842 and was invited by the Commissioners to design Birkenhead Park and Flaybrick Hill Cemetery, although his plans for the cemetery were never used, but when William Jackson built Claughton Manor, it was Paxton who designed the extensive grounds.

Through his interests in railways he became a Director of the Chester and Birkenhead Railway Company and entered Parliament in 1854 representing Coventry for eleven years. When he died in 1865 he was buried at Edensor, the village on the Chatsworth estate.

Edward Kemp was born in London in 1818 and trained as a gardener at Chatsworth under Joseph Paxton. After Paxton's plans for Birkenhead Park had been accepted he was engaged by the Commissioners to supervise the laying out of the Park which entailed not only the purchase of plants and trees, but the supervision of a workforce of about 1000 labourers. After the Park was completed he became Park Superintendent with free accomodation in Italian Lodge, a post he held for forty-six years.

Kemp became a well known landscape gardener achieving an enviable reputation and in 1861 won a competition to design the cemetery at Flaybrick Hill. Throughout his lifetime he designed many private gardens, parks and cemeteries.

After about fifteen years at Italian Lodge he moved to a new house in Park Road West, now number 74. The house still bears a plaque with his and his wife's initials plus the date, E S K 1859. He died there in 1891 and is buried at Flaybrick Hill.

Lewis Hornblower was born in 1823 and was articled to a firm of architects in Liverpool. On Paxton's recommendation he was appointed, at a salary of two guineas per week, to supervise the building of the Lodges in the Park. However he did more than that because he designed the boathouse, bridges, railings, gates and the imposing main entrance.

Hornblower's association with the Park ended with its completion, but he established his own successful business as architect and surveyor, first in Birkenhead and later in Liverpool. He continued to live in Birkenhead where he was a well known figure and when he died in 1879, was buried at Flaybrick Hill.

Harold Rathbone, 1858-1929, established a pottery in Birkenhead, near Hamilton Square, in 1894, and greatly influenced by the Italian School he named his work after the Florentine sculptor Della Robbia. Although a man of outstanding artistic ability who produced ceramics of unusual quality, he lacked business acumen and by 1906 was in such financial difficulties he was forced to close down the pottery. The Williamson Art Gallery has a very fine collection of Della Robbia.

Arthur H. Lee established his tapestry works in Stanley Road, in 1908, where he produced such outstanding furnishing fabrics and hand embroidered tapestries that they were exported to countries throughout the world. The works closed some years ago, but the Williamson Art Gallery houses an interesting collection illustrating the manufacture of these beautiful products.

Philip Wilson Steer O.M. was born in Grange Mount in 1860 and became an internationally famous artist with a distinctly English style. He died in 1942 and a number of his paintings are in the Williamson Art Gallery.

Sir Lewis Casson was born in Alfred Road in 1875 and achieved a distinguished career in the theatre. He married the famous actress Sybil Thorndike in 1908.

F.E. Smith was one of Birkenhead's most illustrious sons. Born on 12th July 1872 at 8 Pilgrim Street, he attended Birkenhead School and Wadham College, Oxford. His father, Fred Smith, was a well known personality in the town who became a prosperous estate agent, then a barrister and in civic life an Alderman and at an early age Mayor, but tragically after one month in office he died in 1888.

F.E. was called to the bar in 1899 and practised in Liverpool from 1902-6 when he entered Parliament as the member for the Walton Division of Liverpool. It was said that he inherited his gifts of rhetoric and repartee from his father and after a brilliant maiden speech, his parliamentary success was assured. In 1915 he became Solicitor General, then Attorney General and from 1919-22 Lord Chancellor. He was knighted in 1918 and after successive honours became the first Earl of Birkenhead in 1922. He died in 1928.

James L. Garvin C.H. was born in Birkenhead at 117 Saint Anne Street and attended Saint Laurence's School. He was only a child when his father, a seaman, was drowned and his mother had to take in washing to support her family. The young James worked first for the Liverpool Post and Echo, became a journalist and eventually a famous editor of the Observer. He died in January 1947.

Henry Cohen was another of Birkenhead's brilliant sons. Born in Claughton Road in 1900 he attended Saint John's School where he gained a scholarship to Birkenhead Institute, later reading medicine at Liverpool University and the University of Paris. One of the most distinguished medical practitioners in the country, his achievements, honours and appointments, were impressive. Knighted in 1949 he became a Baron in 1956 taking the title Lord Cohen of Birkenhead. He was keenly interested in the Liverpool Playhouse of which he was Chairman for many years and where he could often be seen among the audience. He died in 1977.

Wilfred Owen was born in Oswestry in 1893. When his father was appointed Stationmaster at Woodside Station in 1898 the family moved to Birkenhead where he attended Birkenhead Institute. After leaving the University of London he enlisted in the army and served in the Manchester Regiment. In 1917 he was invalided home and while in hospital wrote many of the poems which expressed his horror of war and its futile waste of life. After returning to his regiment in 1918 he was awarded the Military Cross, but was killed in action on 4th November, one week before the Armistice, aged 25 years.

Considered to be the most important of the war poets of the First World War, potentially great, he described himself as a "poet's poet" and the quality of his poems was recognised by, and won the esteem of, his contemporaries Sassoon, Graves and Auden.

Andrew C. Irvine and George Leigh Mallory were members of the Mount Everest Expedition of 1924 and both perished in their unsuccessful attempt to reach the summit. Andrew Irvine came from Birkenhead and streets named after them record their memory.

Lionel Gamlin is still remembered as a B.B.C. announcer. He was educated at Birkenhead School and Cambridge University. After teaching for some years he joined the B.B.C. in 1936. He died in 1967.

In the contemporary world of entertainment a number of Birkonians have achieved fame on stage, screen and radio.

Megs Jenkins was born in Birkenhead and educated at Claughton College. She was with the Liverpool Playhouse Company from 1933-37 and became well known for her appearances in films and on television.

Patricia Routledge attended Birkenhead High School and read English at Liverpool Univeristy. After a period at Liverpool Playhouse she showed her versatility and skill in revue, television, films and radio, achieving success in each medium.

Valerie Masterson attended Holt Hill Convent and after joining the D'Oyly Carte Opera Company became its principal soprano. She is now an international singer of repute who occasionally makes welcome appearances on British television.

Lewis Collins, born in Gautby Road, is Birkenhead's most recent contribution to the theatrical profession to achieve fame. He has starred in a number of successful television presentations including "The Cuckoo Waltz", "The Professionals" and "Who Dares Wins".

8

Facts and Figures

1150 Hamon de Massie established the Benedictine Priory.
1275 Edward 1st visited the Priory.
1277 Edward 1st again visited the Priory.
1318 A Royal Charter enabled the Monks to build a Guest House.
 1330 By Royal Charter the Monks gained sole right of ferriage from Birkenhead to Liverpool.
1536 The Dissolution of the Monasteries.
1544 Ralph Worsley purchased the Priory and its lands.
1573 Ralph Worsley died. Thomas Powell became Lord of the Manor.
1643 Royalist troops occupied Birket Hall and the woods surrounding it.
1644 Cromwell's troops defeated the Royalists. Birket Hall partially destroyed.
1713 The Priory and estates sold to John Cleveland.
1716 John Cleveland died.
1724 Francis Price became Lord of the Manor.
1762 A six horse coach ran from Woodside to Chester.
1786 The Old Chester Road became a Turnpike Road.
1790 The embankment across Tranmere Pool brought the Chester Road into Birkenhead.
1801 Population 110.
1811 Population 105.
1815 The paddle boat Elizabeth steamed up the Mersey.
 1817 The first steam ferry boat, Etna, sailed from Liverpool to Birkenhead.
1821 Population 200.
 1822 A steam ferry service commenced from Woodside.
1822 Saint Mary's Church opened.
1824 William Laird opened his yard at Wallasey Pool.
1826 William Laird engaged Gillespie Graham.
1828 Laird's built their first iron vessel.

1831 Population 2569.
1833 The First Improvement Act:—
Commissioners appointed
Claughton-cum-Grange joined to Birkenhead
Police Force established
First Market built
Laird's built their first paddle steamer.
1834 Woodside Royal Mail Ferry Hotel built.
1835 The Woodside Ferry Company bought Woodside Ferry.
1840 The Birkenhead to Chester Railway opened.
William Jackson established the Gas Works.
1841 Population 8223.
1842 The Birkenhead Commissioners purchased Woodside Ferry.
1843 The Spring Hill Water Works opened.
Birket Hall demolished.
1844 William Jackson became Lord of the Manor.
The foundation stone of the Docks laid.
Work commenced on the Park.
The Railway tunnel to Monks Ferry under construction.
1845 The new Market Hall opened.
Abattoirs were built.
1847 The first Docks were opened.
The Park opened.
1851 Population 24,285.
1853 Graving Docks constructed between Woodside and Monks Ferry.
1854 Great Western Railway opened a through route from Birkenhead to London.
1856 Public Library established.
Lairds transferred to the river front.
1857 Formation of Mersey Docks and Harbour Board.
1858 Lairds built their first steel ship.
1860 Street Tramway started.
1861 Birkenhead became a Parliamentary Borough incorporating Tranmere, Oxton and Claughton.
John Laird elected first Member of Parliament.
Population — Birkenhead 35,929. Total population of new Borough — 50,101.
Birkenhead elected a Board of Guardians.
A floating landing stage erected at Woodside.
1862 The Alabama launched by Lairds.

1863 The Tranmere Workhouse built.
1864 The Borough Hospital opened.
A new Public Library built in Hamilton Street.
1866 The Alfred Dock opened.
1868 Corn warehouses built on the East Float.
1869 The Children's Hospital started.
1870 The School of Art given by John Laird.
1871 Population — Birkenhead 42,997; Tranmere 16,143; Oxton 2,610; Claughton 2,437.
1874 John Laird died.
1876 Sir William Jackson died.
1877 Charter of Incorporation. Birkenhead became a Borough.
First elections held for a Town Council.
John Laird Junior elected the first Mayor.
The Wallasey Dock opened.
1878 Woodside Station opened.
1879 The floating roadway and landing stage for luggage boats constructed.
The Lairages built.
1881 Population 84,006.
The Corporation acquired Thurstaston Common.
1882 Argyle Street South Baths opened.
Birkenhead granted a Court of Quarter Sessions.
1883 Foundation stone of the Town Hall laid.
The Children's Hospital opened.
1885 Mersey Park opened.
1886 The Mersey Railway opened.
1887 The Town Hall opened.
The Sessions Building opened.
1888 Birkenhead created a County Borough.
1891 Population 99,857.
1893 School Board appointed.
1894 The first Branch Libraries opened.
1895 The Central Fire Station opened.
The River Mersey froze during the great frost.
1897 Bidston Hill acquired by the Corporation.
New Ferry ferry service re-commenced.
1899 Rock Ferry ferry service re-commenced.
1900 Livingstone Street Baths opened.

1901 Population 110,915.
  Electric Trams in Birkenhead.
  The Town Hall partially destroyed by fire.
  Victoria Park opened.
1902 The School Board was replaced by the Education Committee.
1903 Hamilton Square Gardens were opened to the public.
  The Mersey Railway electrified.
1907 General Post Office moved to Argyle Street.
1908 The Boy Scout Movement inaugurated in Birkenhead.
1909 Vittoria Dock constructed.
1911 Population 130,794.
1912 The Clock Tower erected to the memory of King Edward VII.
1913 Tranmere Infirmary opened.
1919 The first motor buses in Birkenhead.
1921 Population 147,577.
  Alwen Reservoir began to supply water to the town.
1925 The Cenotaph unveiled.
  Work began on the Mersey Tunnel — Queensway.
1927 Arrowe Park bought by the Corporation.
  Birkenhead celebrated the Jubilee of the Borough 1877-1927.
1928 The Borough boundaries extended to include Thingwall, Landican, Prenton and part of Bidston.
  The Williamson Art Gallery and Museum opened.
1929 World Jamboree of Boy Scouts held in Arrowe Park.
1931 Population 147,946.
1932 New Ferry ferry service ended.
1933 Bidston Dock opened.
  Byrne Avenue Baths opened.
  Borough boundaries extended to include Noctorum, Woodchurch, and parts of Arrowe, Bidston and Upton.
1934 Queensway and the Central Library opened by King George V.
1937 The last electric tram replaced by buses.
1939 Rock Ferry ferry service ended.
  Submarine Thetis sank in Liverpool Bay.
  Second World War began on 3rd September.
1941 Birkenhead's most severe air raid — 12th-13th March.
  The luggage boats were discontinued.
1945 Peace celebrations.

1948 The foundation stone laid of the Electricity Power Station, Bromborough.
1950 The foundation stone laid of Birkenhead Technical College by H.M. The Queen.
1951 Population 142,392.
1953 The new Police Headquarters opened.
1955 The Technical College opened.
1960 Tranmere Oil Terminal established.
1961 Population 141,683.
1967 Work begun on Mersey Tunnel Approaches Scheme. Woodside Station closed.
1969 Official opening of the Mersey Tunnel Approaches Scheme.
1970 Saint Mary's Church demolished.
1971 Population 137,738.
Quarter Sessions terminated by Courts Act.
1973 The official opening of the new Fire Station.
1974 Birkenhead became part of the Metropolitan Borough of Wirral.
1978 The extension of the Mersey Railway opened by H.M. Queen Elizabeth II.
1982 Arrowe Park Hospital opened.
1986 Merseyside County Council abolished.
Police now part of the Merseyside Police Authority.
Fire Services now known as Merseyside Fire and Civil Defence Authority.

Bibliography

The History of the Hundred of Wirral, William Williams Mortimer.
Birkenhead 1877-1974.
History of the County Palatine and City of Chester, Ormerod.
From Priory to Polaris, Stella M. Pinches.
The Set of the Sails, Margery Griffiths.
Wirral – Yesterday – Today and Tomorrow, The Wirral Society.
Birkenhead – Yesterday and Today, W.R.S. McIntyre.
Memories of Birkenhead, H. Gamlin.
Twixt Mersey and Dee, H. Gamlin.
The Search for Old Wirral, David Randall.
Bygone Birkenhead, J.R. Kaighin.
History of Birkenhead, Sulley.
Birkenhead in its Infancy, H. Salt.
Auld Lang Syne, H.B. Neilson.
Milestones of History, Readers' Digest.
Liverpool, George Chandler.
The Age of Plunder, W.G. Hoskins.
Reminiscences of Birkenhead, Charles Grey Mott.
Birkenhead and its Surroundings, H.K. Aspinall.
The Wirral Peninsular, Norman Ellison.
A History of Great Britain, R.B. Mowat.
Outline Plan for the County Borough of Birkenhead, Sir Charles Reilly and N.J. Aslan.
Various old maps.